POMPEIANA.

THE

TOPOGRAPHY, EDIFICES, AND ORNAMENTS

OF

POMPEII.

BY

SIR WILLIAM GELL, F.R.S. F.S.A.,

AND

JOHN P. GANDY,

ARCHITECT.

THIRD EDITION.

1852.

Copyright © 2013 Read Books Ltd.
This book is copyright and may not be
reproduced or copied in any way without
the express permission of the publisher in writing

British Library Cataloguing-in-Publication Data
A catalogue record for this book is available from the
British Library

A Short Introduction to the History of Pompeii

Pompeii was an ancient Roman town-city near the modern Italian city of Naples. It is famed for being one of the ill-feted settlements destroyed and buried by the massive eruption of Mount Vesuvius in 79 AD. Along with Herculaneum, Pompeii is of particular interest and historical importance due to its preservation under the several metres of volcanic ash and pumice, protecting it from air and moisture. This created a snapshot of a moment in an ancient civilisation that would otherwise have been eroded by time.

It is believed to have been founded by Osci in the sixth or seventh century BC. By the 4th century it was under the control of the Roman Empire, finally being conquered and becoming a Roman colony in 80 BC following an unsuccessful rebellion against the Republic. At the time of its destruction, Pompeii had a population of around 11,000 and a well developed infrastructure comprising a port, an amphitheatre, a gymnasium, and a complex water system.

The first evidence of the demise of this settlement came in the form of a letter written by Pliny the Younger, the Roman, lawyer, author, and magistrate. In the letter he describes the death of his uncle, Pliny the Elder, an admiral of the Roman fleet, and his demise while trying to rescue the citizens of Pompeii. However, it was not until 1599, when a channel was being dug to divert the river Samo, that the entombed settlement was re-discovered. Domenica Fonatana, a Swiss architect, was called in for his opinion on the finding. He uncovered several frescoes but then decided to cover them over again. Nobody knows exactly why he did this – some see it as a forward-thinking act of preservation, while others contend that the sexual content of many of the works may not have been considered 'good taste' during the counter-reformation period.

If it was an act of censorship then he was certainly not alone in his opinion. When King Francis of Naples visited the Pompeii exhibition at the national Gallery in 1819, he was so embarrassed at being exposed to the artwork, while in the company of his wife and daughter, that he ordered some of it to be locked away in a secret cabinet for the eyes of "people of mature age and respected morals" only. After being opened and closed again several times over the next two hundred years the exhibit reopened in 2000, but it is still not allowed to be viewed by minors unless in the presence of a guardian or with written permission. Aside from the art of the lost city, many other aspects of ancient life were also preserved, such as clothes, coins, furniture, food, and the bodies of the unfortunate residents. Previously it was thought that they had been killed by ash suffocation, but recent testing indicates that they died an instant death from the searing heat of the eruption.

Pompeii is now a hugely popular tourist destination and a UNESCO heritage site. Since the town's excavation however, its exposure to the elements has led to much erosion and many of the buildings are in dire need of restoration. Conservation of such a site is both time consuming and expensive, and an estimated $335 million is needed for the necessary repair work. Pompeii provides us with a fascinating window into the daily lives of an ancient civilisation though, and with one third of the city still to be uncovered, is likely to continue presenting us with yet more insights into a culture frozen in time.

PREFACE.

As early as the year 1684, some unusual circumstances in sinking a well had excited the observation of those who, unknowingly, cultivated the soil immediately above the theatre of the ancient city of Herculaneum. In the *Istoria Universale* of Bianchini, 1699, we have an account of the strata pierced; from which it appears, that after a bed, 10 feet thick, of cultivable soil, ten alternating courses of lava and earth, or tufa, were passed, before finding the water at the depth of 90 feet, or 18 below the ancient level at that spot; although it may be remarked, that various inscriptions, and pieces of wrought iron, had been found at 22 feet below the surface. The Prince D'Elbœuf, who had been sent at the head of an imperial army to Naples, and had married a native princess, about 1706 began a palace upon the spot, possessed himself of the well, and the marbles extracted were pounded into terras, or scagliola, for the floors of the new building. Some statues discovered were sent to France, his native country, or Vienna, to Prince Eugene, under whom he had served. We believe it was not until the year 1736 that the operations, suspended by the interference of the government, were renewed by the king, and the ancient name of the city correctly ascertained: but the great depth of incumbent matter scarcely admitted the possibility of leaving any part open; so that even the architectural decoration was removed, and some of the columns of the scene of the theatre were employed in the church of St. Januarius at Naples.

This latter circumstance presents a great feature in comparing the respective merits of the two cities. Architecture will be but little illustrated in the gloomy caverns of Herculaneum, though its statues and bronzes are restored in many instances perfect. Statues, or bronzes, are more rarely found at Pompeii; but in the mind of the liberal antiquary, the loneliness of its ruin may be animated by learned recollection, while its dignity may recall the image of ancient riches, industry, or magnificence.

Pompeii was begun upon in 1748; and it may at first excite our surprise, that from this date to the present day, no work has appeared in the English language upon the subject of its domestic antiquities, except a few pages by Sir William Hamilton, in the Archæologia.

Subsequently to the discovery of the two theatres, the Greek temple, those of Isis and of Æsculapius, the great gate, the villa, and some of the sepulchres, the French, during their occupation of Naples, laid open the walls[1] around the city, the greater portion of the Street of the Tombs,[1] with the Forum and Basilica: and the re-clearing the Amphitheatre was also commenced.

At this period, under the particular and liberal patronage of Madame Murat,[2] Mons. Mazois, who had lived some time almost upon the spot, began his splendid work; which promises, if ever finished, to leave little to be desired upon the subject of the architectural details or ornaments: while the magnificent volumes of the Academy of Naples, aided by the munificence of the court, had already made known the principal objects in the Royal Museum. Of these the original catalogue of 1755 gave 738 pictures, 350 statues, and 1647 minor pieces.

In the mean time, the subject had not failed to excite the research of the learned, though their dissertations

---

[1] The walls in October, 1812; the tombs in the March following.

[2] This patronage, we believe, consisted of fifteen thousand francs.

have sometimes been but little calculated for our instruction. Amongst the most prominent are the two thick quartos of Monsignore O. A. Bayardi; at the close of whose second volume, Hercules is still employed upon the labours which preceded his arrival in the Campi Phlegræi, and consequently had not yet thought of laying the foundation of either of our cities.

With these it cannot be the intention of the authors of the present work to compete: they have, therefore, generally avoided entering into a scrupulous detail of measurement, aware that those who feel sufficiently interested to inquire the precise dimensions of any object would prefer the larger volumes as books of reference, though their bulk renders them unfit for the traveller, and their costliness unattainable to many who would value them most.

The two general plans of the city will give an exact idea of what has been already effected, what yet remains to be performed by the excavators, as well as the progress made since this work was begun: for his Sicilian majesty still continues to employ as many labourers as the finances of the country will permit; and as the excavations are conducted in a regular manner, rather with the laudable intention of laying open the city than of searching for treasures, every day will add to the knowledge already acquired on this most interesting but almost inexhaustible subject.

To those who have not the opportunity of passing much time upon the spot, it is presumed this work may be useful, in enabling them to select such objects as they may think most worth their attention. The distance from Naples is about thirteen miles; and the Soldiers' Quarters, as one of the porticoes is vulgarly called, is the spot whence strangers usually set out to make their observations. Those who, following this work, would begin at the Street of the Tombs, should drive to the Villa Suburbana; accessible to carriages by a lane turning from the main road, before arriving at the little taverna, or inn. Cicerone, or guides, are always on the spot ready to accompany the traveller. They are usually civil, honest, and intelligent. Indeed, it is but doing justice to the peasants who cultivate the soil of Pompeii to state, that notwithstanding the character commonly given to the Neapolitans by strangers, they are a most harmless and inoffensive race.

Manuscripts have been found only in Herculaneum. Yet it may be proper here to make some slight record upon the subject. In a letter of 1755, from Signor Paderni, keeper of the Royal Museum, inserted in the 'Philosophical Transactions,' we have a short account of the discovery of a room, paved with mosaic, and containing presses, in which were 355 volumes, of which 18 were Latin. But the whole number found is from 1500 to 1800, principally Greek. Many fell to pieces, and some were destroyed before their value was discovered: for they generally bear the appearance of burnt pieces of wood, about two inches diameter, and from six to eight inches long. The writing is in one row of columns, side by side, beginning in the centre of the roll, and containing from twenty to thirty short lines in a column. The time and assiduous caution required, render the unrolling them an operation of tedious difficulty, not hitherto rewarded by the discovery of any work of consequence; though the learned world must ever feel grateful to the munificence of his present Majesty George IV,[1] to whose liberality they are partly indebted for the progress already made in developing these invaluable relics. Sir Humphry Davy has more recently succeeded in detaching some of the rolls by a chemical process; but it appears that the damp having penetrated both in ancient and modern times, the ink, which was nothing more than carbon and water, had generally disappeared from those submitted to his process.

It may be right to notice the assertion of a popular periodical work, "that Herculaneum and Pompeii were not overwhelmed suddenly and at the same time." The learned author of the article seems to have forgotten, that the destruction of the cities, alluded to by Dio, did not take place till fourteen years after the death of Seneca, whom he quotes, and who refers only to the earthquake of 63. — (See *Edin. Review,* vol. xvi, 383.)

The authors have to acknowledge the kind assistance of ROBERT COCKEREL, Esq., by whom they were favoured with the plan of the house of Pansa, and the loan of drawings of the paintings in Plates 42 and 43. For a

---

[1] Preface to the first Edition, 1817.

great part of the plan of the Forum, Plate 44, they are indebted to R. SHARP, Esq.

It may be proper to state, that the original drawings for this work were made with the *camera lucida,* by Sir WILLIAM GELL. To render the subject clearer, a slight alteration has in two or three instances been made, but always mentioned in the text. The literary part, with the exception of the first essay, is by his coadjutor.

FRONTISPIECE.

The Frontispiece is wholly compiled from paintings and bronzes found at Pompeii. The figure reading a volume, the chair upon which she sits, the footstool, and scrinium, or capsa, for manuscripts, at her feet. The marble table, and implements for writing; the pavement, and distant building, are all from the same source.

The three bronzes are amongst the most beautiful discovered: they are of Mercury, Cupid, and Venus. The latter has annulets of gold on her arms and legs.

The brazier with four towers was contrived to heat water or liquors, as well as to warm the room. The charcoal was placed in the square part, which was lined with iron. The towers held the liquid: their lids were raised by rings. The whole was 2 feet 1 inch square.

Glass, as used in windows for the transmission of light, was almost unknown at Pompeii: indeed, two hundred years later, we find Vopiscus numbering this luxury amongst the extravagancies of the merchant Firmus, whose riches enabled him for some time to contest the sovereignty of Egypt with the troops of Aurelian.

The relievo representing Caryatides is from the Royal Museum.

by John Martin. Engraved by W.B. Cooke.

ERUPTION OF VESUVIUS,
From the Sea.

MOUNT VESUVIUS.
OVER THE PLAIN & CITY OF POMPEII.

MOUNT VESUVIUS, OVER THE PLAIN AND CITY OF POMPEII.

The site of Pompeii, under Vesuvius, is marked by the long light line formed by the ashes turned out of the excavations: upon this the Amphitheatre is the farthest object to the right; while behind the left extremity is the gate of Herculaneum. More to the left, on the slope of the mountain beyond Torre del Annunziata, is Camaldoli della Torre, a hill of pumice. Four craters occur between it and the summit. Nearly under the farthest, to the right, are some mills, on the Sarnus.

The four craters were thrown up during the eruption of 1760, when twelve mouths opened at the foot of the mountain, and kept up a noise like a continued discharge of artillery from as many batteries. The torrent of lava, which, 300 feet wide and 15 feet thick, reached within a few hundred yards of the sea, is crossed, leaving these craters on the left, before entering Torre del Annunziata.

The account, by the *Padre della Torre*, of this lava, in its approach to a building, is curious. He informs us, that at eight or nine inches from the wall it stopped, and swelled, environing the house without at first touching it; which he attributes to the density of the fiery vapour emitted by the fused material: but if a wooden door occurred, it was instantly reduced to ashes, and the torrent entered the house.

The villages of Bosco Reale and Bosco Tre Case are hardly distinguishable under the crater of Vesuvius.

In another part of this work it has been said, that ruins of the city must always have appeared above the soil: with reference to that opinion we may recollect, that Pompeii was called by the first excavators Civita, a name the spot seems to have borne some centuries previously, and which it probably had borne from the time of its destruction.

Upon a remark of Colonel Squire, that "the plural termination of some Greek cities, as Athens, Thebes, &c. refers to their united portions; the upper with the citadel and the lower town;" the learned editor of a volume of *Journals of Travellers in the Levant* cites a parallel passage from Bishop Lowth, who had explained, that Sion and Jerusalem might be meant in the plural form used by the prophet Isaiah, lxiv, 10. The instances are, perhaps, but few: Pompeii is certainly an exception; and we may recollect that islands are sometimes so designated. This remark is, however, ingenious.

It would be difficult to decide upon the relative magnitude of Pompeii with Herculaneum: yet, from the lead its name takes in ancient authors, the former must, in all probability, have been the most populous. Its situation was favoured by the residence of Cicero, and by the son of the emperor Claudius, who there died by swallowing a pear.

The building in the foreground with a tower is a farmhouse.

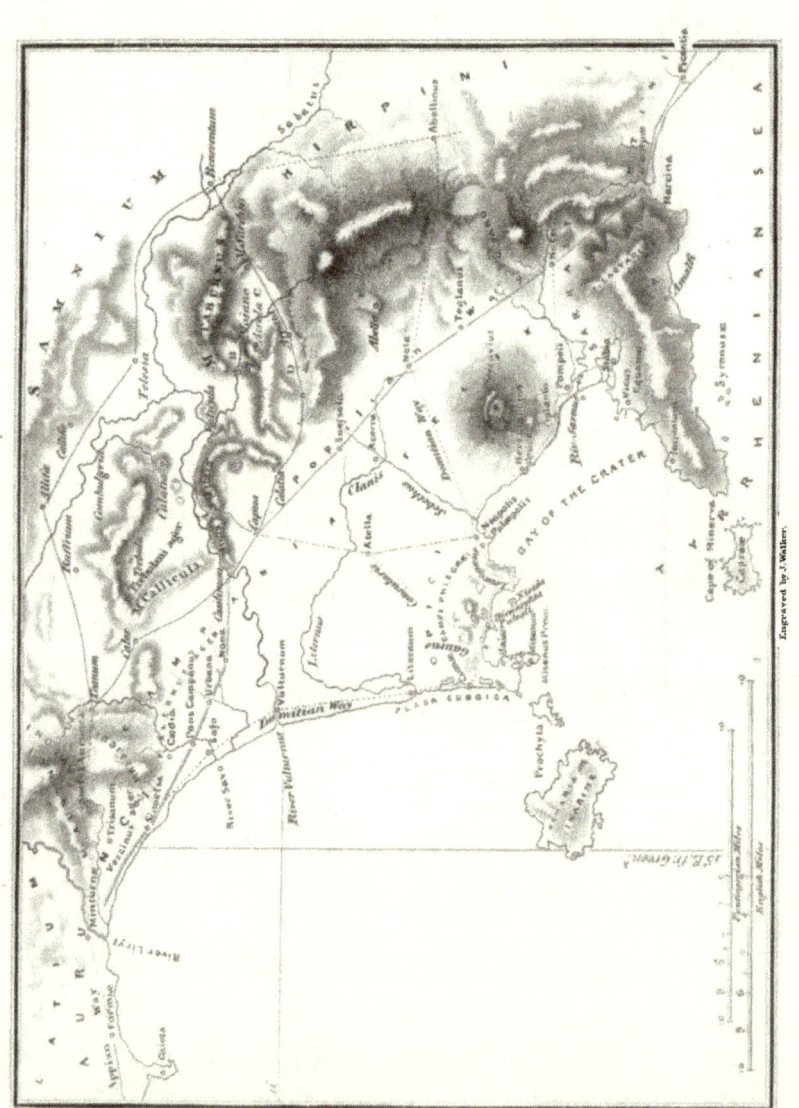

POMPEII.
TERRITORY OF THE CAMPANIANS.

MAP OF CAMPANIA.

This map is grounded upon the modern survey of Zannoni, considered the most correct that has been made of the country. The learned dissertation of Pellegrini upon its localities has been the guide in fixing the ancient names; and the Peutingerian tables have at the same time been consulted.[1]

The proper boundary of Campania may yet afford subject for controversy, since we find it varying in each successive age, as well as with every writer. Hannibal, according to Polybius, thought it in form like a theatre, surrounded by impracticable mountains, which left but three ways into the Campi Phlegræi, as he designates the plain between its principal cities, Nola and Capua.

Behind Tifata, that general for some time maintained his head quarters; but its luxuries proved fatal to the discipline of his armies. As the early existence of Rome was fought for on these plains, five centuries and a half before the Christian æra, so at an equal period after that epoch were they the theatre of a contest for its possession, after Rome had ceased to struggle. During two months, the Draco or Sarnus divided the contending armies, until Teias, the Gothic king, retired to Mount Lactarius, where he was defeated and slain by the eunuch Narses. With

[1] The alterations in this edition are from personal inspection.

that war ended the existence of the last assembly pretending to the name of a Roman senate.

This delightful region, the "pompa maggior della natura," says Micali, was ever considered, for its soft climate and fertile soil, the compendium of all the prerogatives of Italy. Its wines, its roses, its vases, were equally celebrated; though its diseases should not be forgotten in ancient or modern times.

Ptolemy bounds Campania by the Lirys and Sarnus. Frontinus tells us, it was longer than broad. The greatest length, according to this map, from Sinuessa to the Sarnus, will be found to measure 33 English miles: the breadth, from Tifata and the continuant line of mountains to the sea, will average 12; producing an area of 396 English square miles, each containing about 127 Roman jugera. We shall thus find the superficial content of this country precisely agreeing with the 50,000 jugera assigned to it by Cicero, in his letter to Atticus, ii, 16. The ancient coast, from Oplontis to Stabia, seems to have receded on either side of Pompeii; and modern observation would point out the west as well as the south sides of the city as formerly washed by the sea, which turned the amphitheatre before the Sarnus fell in. The lands of Nuceria joined the sea, according to Pliny; which explains the circumstance of Cornelius landing at Pompeii to lay them waste. But a strong proof that Pompeii had no secure station for ships may be cited in the conduct of Hannibal, whose existence in Campania depended upon his procuring possession of one of its ports. Foiled at Naples, he took Nuceria, a city in some respects connected with Pompeii;[1] but he evidently never looked upon the latter as possessing the advantage he sought.

The Sarnus is now within a third of a mile of Pompeii. It rises from a fountain at the pretty village called by its name, at the foot of the hills between Nola and Nocera, and runs in a clear as well as rapid stream through the neighbouring level, the "dulcis Pompeia palus vicina salinis Herculeis" of Columella. It is about the magnitude of the Cam, a little above Cambridge. Rivegliano, the "Herculis petra," is very little distant from its mouth, and consists of two or three rocks, with a neglected castle.

It would be difficult to imagine the origin of the name assigned to this river during the middle ages, unless, indeed, Draco could be supposed a renewal of a more ancient appellation, suggested by its winding course.

The Peutingerian tables give upon the Appian Way the following distances:

Formiæ to Minturnæ, 8; Sinuessa, 8; Pons Campanus, 7; Urbana, 3; Nona, 3; Casilinum, 5; Capua, 3; Galatia, 6; Novæ, 6; Caudium, 8; Beneventum, 11.

Beneventum, leaving the Appian Road, to Abellinus, 16; to Icentia, 12; to Salernum, 12.

Casilinum to Cales, 7; to Teanum, 3.

Capua to Atella, 8; to Naples, 8.

Atella, or Capua, to Suessola, 8; Nola, 8; Teglanus, 5;—Nuceria, 8; Salernum, 8.

Capua to Temple of Diana, 3; Saticula, 6; Telesia, 6.

Naples to Herclanium, 6; Oplontis, 6; Pompeii, 3.

Nuceria to Pompeii, or Stabia, 12; perhaps 7.

As the supposed date of these tables is as late as the

[1] They had a common amphitheatre, and, perhaps, lands in common.

reign of Theodosius, or the close of the fourth century, we may either imagine the inaccuracies of the latter four distances to have arisen from the undetermined sites of the lost cities, or admit this curious document as evidence that their ruins still pointed out their places to its constructors.

PLAN OF THE CITY,

AS EXCAVATED TO APRIL, 1819.

As the several portions of this are given upon a larger and more detailed scale at Plates II, XXVII, XXXIV, XLIV, LXIV, it becomes unnecessary to repeat here the explanation, which may be found with the respective plans.

A few of the letters of reference, which are not clearly distinguishable upon Plate I, are here repeated.

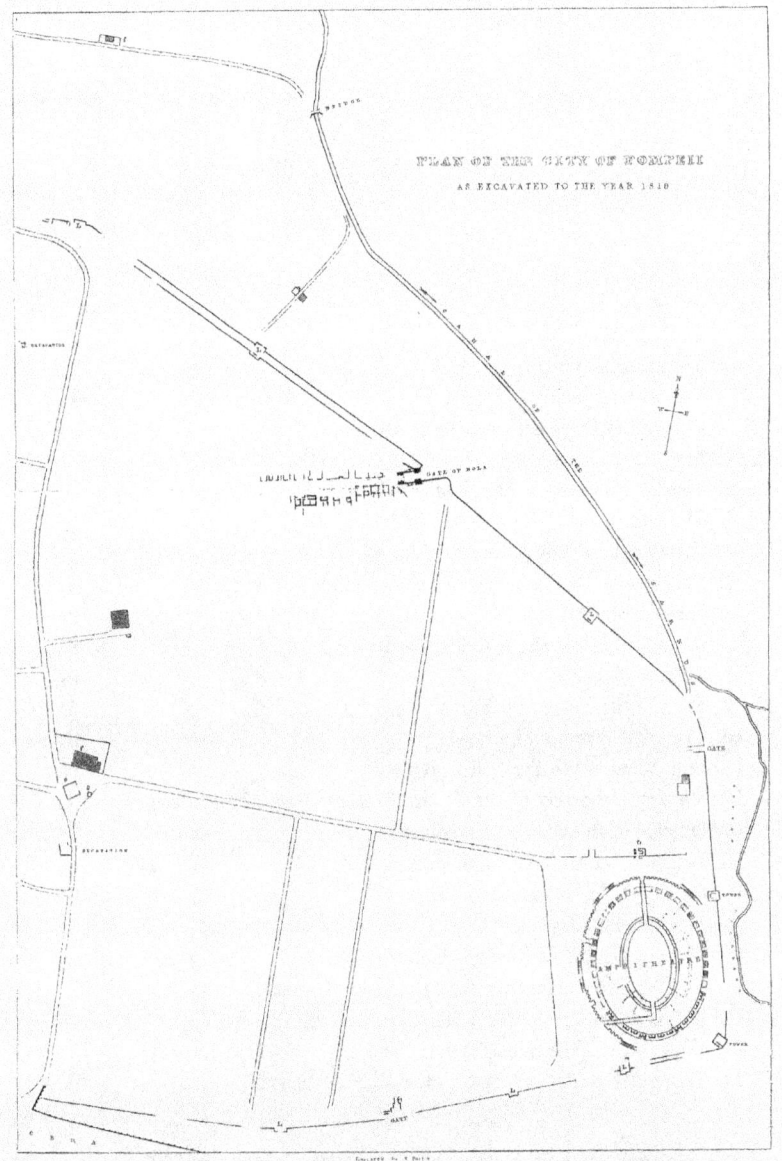

LIST OF THE PLATES.

	PAGE
FRONTISPIECE	i
View of Pompeii	xi
Map of Campania	xiii
Plan of the City, as excavated to 1821[1]	xvi
1. Excavated City of Pompeii, to the year 1817	11
2. Plan of the Street of the Tombs	67
3. View up to the Street of the Tombs	79
4. View of the Inside of the Triclinium	81
5. Entrance to the Tomb of Naevoleia Tyche	ib.
6. Interior of the Tomb of Naevoleia	ib.
7. View across the Street of the Tombs	82
8. Tomb of Scaurus	ib.
9. Back of the Tomb of Scaurus	84
10. Insulated Tomb, uninscribed	ib.
11. Side View of the Tomb of C. Quietus	85
12. View in the Street of the Tombs, from the Gate of Herculaneum	ib.
13. Outside of the Gate of Herculaneum	94
14. Inside of the Gate of Herculaneum	ib.
15. Gate of Nola, outside	95
16. Walls of the City	96
17. View of one of the Towers, from the Outside	ib.
18. Various Ornaments from near the Gate of Nola	97
19. Entrance to the City from Herculaneum, restored	98
20. View in the Villa Suburbana	118
21. Triangular Room and Bath in the Villa Suburbana	ib.

[1] In the first edition, this plan only went so far as April, 1819.

		PAGE
22.	View of the Junction of Two Streets	119
23.	View in the House of the Vestals	ib.
24.	Painting in the House of the Vestals	120
25.	Court of the House of Surgical Instruments	ib.
26.	Pictures and Ornaments	121
27.	Plan of the House of Sallust, called of Actæon	ib.
28.	Atrium of the House of Sallust	124
29.	Restoration of the Atrium of Sallust	125
30.	House of Sallust, Side of a Room	126
31.	Painting, Tiles, and Ornaments	ib.
32.	Pseudo-Garden and Triclinium	127
33.	House of Actæon, Ornaments, Paintings, &c.	128
34.	Plan of the House of Pansa	ib.
35.	Entrance to the House of Pansa	134
36.	Peristyle, or Inner Court, of the House of Pansa	135
37.	Restoration of the Atrium in the House of Pansa	ib.
38.	Oven and Mills in the House of Pansa	136
39.	Tetrastyle Cavædium in the House S. of the Basilica	138
40.	Side of a Room	ib.
41.	Side of a Room	ib.
42.	Picture from the Excavation of Queen Caroline	139
43.	Painting from the same Excavation	140
44.	Plan of the Forum and Basilica	150
45.	General View of the Forum and Basilica	159
46.	View of the Forum and Basilica	160
47.	View in the Forum	ib.
48.	View of the Forum from the Temple of Jupiter	ib.
49.	South End of the Forum, restored	161
50.	Ornaments from the Basilica	ib.
51.	View of the Temple at the North End of the Forum	167
52.	North End of the Forum, restored	ib.
53.	View of the Temple of Bacchus	168
54.	View of the Temple of Bacchus, looking towards Vesuvius	169
55, 56.	Paintings	ib.
57, 58.	Paintings in the Temple of Bacchus	170
59.	Painting at the Temple of Bacchus	171
60.	Painting at the Temple of Bacchus	ib.
61.	Painting	172
62.	Painting	ib.

		PAGE
63. View of the New Temple, East Side of the Forum	.	. 172
64. Plan of the Quarter of the Theatres	. .	. 178
65. Entrance Portico to the Greek Temple	. .	. 189
66. Entrance Portico to the Greek Temple, restored .	.	. 190
67. Remains of the Greek Temple	. . .	. ib.
68. View of the Excavation of the Theatres	. .	. 191
69. View in the Court of the Temple of Isis	. .	. 192
70. View in the Great Theatre, looking towards the Scene .		. 193
71. View of the Back of the Theatre	. . .	. ib.
72. Colonnade below the Great Theatre	. .	. 194
73. View in the Little Theatre .	. . .	. ib.
74. View in the School behind the Great Theatre	.	. 195
75. View in the Amphitheatre	. . .	. 196
76. Painting in the Amphitheatre	. .	. 198
77. Painting of the Twelve Gods	. . .	. ib.

Heap of ashes from the excavations.

The City of Pompeii, distant about thirteen miles from Naples, stood originally upon a rising ground, overlooking a fertile plain, which stretched on one side towards Nola, and on the other to Nuceria and Stabia.

The eminence is at present much increased by the mass of volcanic matter poured upon this ill-fated city by Vesuvius; for while the cinders, which fell upon the fields, have been either decomposed and carried away by subsequent rains, or have only caused an encroachment on the sea; the walls and habitations of the city have served to retain within their circuit all that was discharged upon the spot by the volcano; so that the extent of the buildings is very distinctly marked by the hill, formed of pumice and the gradual accumulation of vegetable earth which covers it.

Pompeii was however always upon a height, as the ascent by the street of the tombs sufficiently proves; and the apparent elevation of the city above the sea must have been anciently much the same as at present; for, as the soil is generally raised but little higher than the top of the lower stories of the houses, the upper apartments and the public buildings might have nearly equalled the trees which now clothe the summit: this eminence seems to have been formed at some very remote period, and is connected with the foot of Vesuvius, from which it may be considered as a sort of promontory stretching into the plain.

It is surprising, that with such a testimony of former devastation as the city of Pompeii before their eyes, and the frequent recurrence of similar ravages, the people of the country should have ventured to erect two large and populous villages three miles nearer the crater of Vesuvius, especially as they invariably evince the greatest alarm when the mountain exhibits any symptoms of an approaching eruption.

An idea has prevailed, that the sea once washed the walls of Pompeii; but though it is said that rings have been found, to which it has been supposed vessels were anciently moored, close to the ruins, yet there seems great reason to believe, that the trade of Pompeii was carried on, as Strabo intimates, by means of the river Sarnus, which yet runs a clear, deep, and navigable river, approaching within a quarter of a mile of the site of the city; the situation rendering it a convenient emporium for the commerce of the cities of Nola, Nuceria, and the produce of the fertile plain south of Vesuvius.

In the Peutingerian tables, the distances of the neighbouring towns are thus stated:

Neapolis to Herculaneum	XI[1]
Herculaneum to Oplontis	VI
Oplontis to Pompeii	III
Pompeii to Nuceria	XII
Oplontis to Stabia	III
Stabia to Pompeii	III

Pompeii is thus made twenty miles distant from Naples; and if no better guide than these very inaccurate tables was consulted, it is not surprising that its true site should have been unknown, even to Cluverius; though a very slight examination of the spot, where a considerable quantity of Roman brickwork was always visible, ought to have enabled him to ascertain it: a peasant, who sinking a well in his garden found some fragments of marble, by accident brought to light Herculaneum, which, buried under accumulated beds of lava, to the depth of above sixty feet, might possibly have remained for ever undiscovered; whereas the ruins of Pompeii might have been observed by any traveller along the road.

No one, however, could have suspected how rich a

[1] This, in the original tables, must be an error for VI.

mine of antiquities existed here, until a labourer, in the middle of the last century, found, in ploughing, a statue of brass; which circumstance being reported to the government, was one of the causes which led to the first excavations; and subsequently the accidental discovery of the temple of Isis, while some workmen were employed in the construction of a subterraneous aqueduct for the use of the manufactory of arms at Torre dell' Annunziata, contributed not a little to confirm the expectations which had been excited. Since that period the operations have always been carrying on, with more or less activity, so that by degrees the whole will be cleared. In the mean time, notwithstanding the great attention which has been bestowed on the preservation of the monuments first found, they are beginning to suffer from the effects of that exposure which has taken place since their second birth. In the short space of time which has elapsed since their discovery, the alternations of winter and summer have generally effaced the paintings, and in many instances entirely stripped every trace of stucco from the walls: the winter months, though mild in comparison with the same season in the north of Europe, are generally accompanied by torrents of rain, which gradually insinuating itself between the bricks and the plaster, loosens and forces off, first indeed small portions, but eventually detaches the whole; so that we are not permitted to hope that the theatres, houses, or temples, constructed as they are of the most perishable materials, can remain for the satisfaction of posterity; and although, in this point of view, it may be considered fortunate for the succeeding generation that the operations proceed so slowly, still too much cannot now be done to preserve the memory of what exists. The fortifications, however, which are in some parts built with solid blocks of stone, may yet remain for many centuries, as the doric temple would have done had it not been destroyed by external force; whereas a short period must suffice to destroy every vestige of the rest of the city, which is built of bricks and rubble work, without any pretension to durability or excellence of construction. The streets are curiously paved, with irregularly-shaped pieces of black volcanic stone, well put together, and generally exhibiting the tracks of wheels. The town was originally founded upon an ancient bed of lava, though there exists no record of an earlier eruption than that which destroyed it.

The gates of the city now visible are five in number; they are known on the spot, by the names of the gate of Herculaneum or Naples, the gate of Vesuvius, the gate of Nola, that of Sarno, and the gate of Stabia: but as these names have been applied since the discovery of the ruins, they must be considered merely as modern appellations; for neither the ruins themselves, nor any existing authority, afford any document for determining their ancient designations.

There may have been other openings of less consequence, communicating with the great street by little passages, which descend to the walls in a part now covered by the rubbish of the excavations; for from the gate of Stabia to that of Naples, a space nearly equal to half the circumference of Pompeii, the city could scarcely be without a considerable outlet; unless the sea, as before mentioned to have been supposed by some, had anciently washed the walls: but none has yet been discovered.

The gate of Nola is the only one of which the arch is preserved: from which circumstance, on a superficial view, it has sometimes been imagined to have been of more consequence than the others, whereas it is in fact of smaller dimensions.

The excavations afford an opportunity of observing, that the ruin of Pompeii was not effected by an uniform shower of cinders or pumice-stones. A section near the amphitheatre gives the general proportions of the mass under which the city is buried to the depth of about twenty feet. Separating the whole into five portions, we shall find the first three to consist of pumice-stone in small pieces, resembling a light white cinder, and covering the pavement to the depth of twelve feet: the next portion is composed of six parts, beginning with a stratum of small black stones, not more than three inches in thickness; to this succeeds a thin layer of mud, or earth which has been mixed with water, and appears to have been deposited in a liquid state; upon this lies another thin stratum of little stones, of a mixed hue, in which blue predominates; a second stratum of mud, separated from a third, by a thin wavy line of mixed blue stones, completes the fourth portion: while the fifth or highest division consists entirely of vegetable earth, principally formed by the gradual decomposition of the volcanic matter from the date of the eruption to the present day.

From the evident agency of water, observable in some of these strata, a theory has been published, which attempts, in spite of history and Vesuvius, to account for the depositions at Pompeii as the effect of alluvion; the natural inference, however, to be drawn from an inspection of the spot seems to be, that the hot pumice-stone fell in successive showers, and not in one mass. Had the latter been the case, the city must indeed have become the tomb of its inhabitants; whereas comparatively few skeletons have been found. The strata of mud were also discharged in a very liquid state from the mountain, an event by no means uncommon during later eruptions; and it is from this circumstance that vaulted passages, of which the covering still remains entire, are usually found as completely full of the deposition as the open courts, or the chambers where the roofs have been consumed.[1]

It will be easy to account for the general disappearance of the upper story, of which the traces often exist, not only in the staircases, but sometimes in the paintings and remaining walls; for the volcanic matter does not appear to have been discharged in sufficient quantity to have buried the whole of the walls of the ground floor, throughout all parts of the city; consequently, whatever rose to a greater height remained a ruin accessible to the surviving proprietors, and liable to the same destruc-

---

[1] The tiles of some roofs are still sometimes found almost in their original positions, borne up by the volcanic matter; while the timber which once supported them has decayed away.

tion from time, or removal of the materials for conversion, as any other neglected building. In many parts of the city, the upper stories still remain; but they seem to have been of very inferior consequence to those on the ground floor.

Many circumstances observable in Pompeii would appear incomprehensible, did we not recollect that the destruction of the city was the work of two distinct periods of calamity; and that the restoration of its buildings, after the great earthquake, was only taking place at the moment of its final extinction. This earthquake, by which Pompeii was almost destroyed, happened, as we are informed by Seneca, in the ninth year of the reign of the emperor Nero,[1] about sixteen years previous to the eruption; and the unfinished state of the repairs in many of the buildings attests the fact.

We are led by one of the sepulchral inscriptions to look for the discovery of a temple of Ceres, as the learned seemed disposed to refer that of the Grecian doric order near the theatre to the worship of Neptune.

It appears to have been sometimes the practice, during the first excavations at Pompeii, to throw into that relinquished, the materials drawn from the next explored, after the paintings, mosaic pavements, and other articles considered valuable, had been removed; but a contrary system was subsequently adopted, and is now acted upon.

---

[1] A.D. 63, U.C. 816.
"Caius Mummius Regulus,
Lucius Virginius Rufus."—Coss.

Although their better preservation was the end consulted in thus transferring these monuments to form a part of a distant collection; still it is much to be regretted that means could not have been devised for their preservation on the precise spot at which they were originally found, and where locality would have thrown around them an interest which they entirely lose when crowded with other curiosities, into the Museums of Portici or Naples.

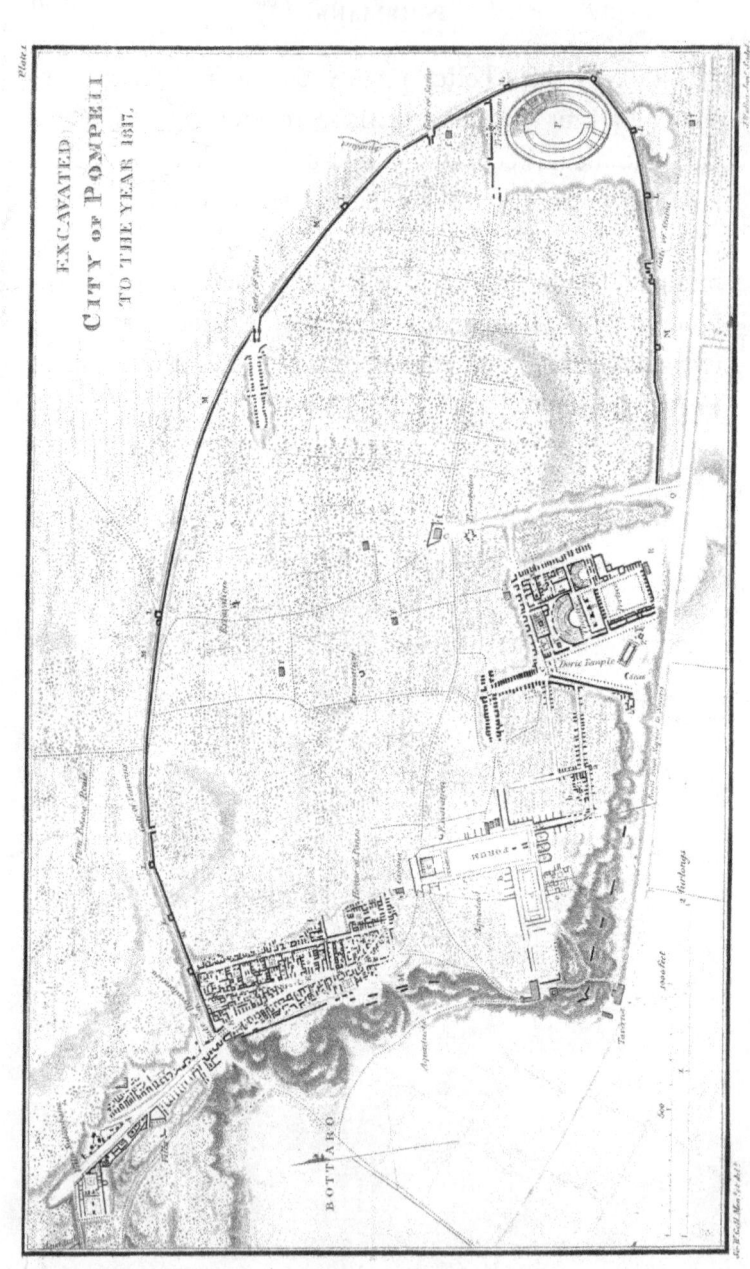

PLATE I.

MAP OF THE CITY OF POMPEII.

The Map of the entire city of Pompeii, as far as the excavations have at present permitted it to be known, is here given; from which the respective situations of the different parts may be understood, and a comparison of what has been hitherto discovered with that which yet remains buried may be drawn.

The city was about 3330 yards in circumference, or nearly two British miles.

- A   Street of the Tombs.
- B C D E F G   Great Street or *Corso* of Pompeii.
- B   Ancient Post House to the left entering the City.
- C C   Fountains.
- D   Passages from the great Street to the Walls.
- E   House, on the left going towards the Forum, commonly called of Actæon, from a painting in it, the subject of which is his metamorphosis.
- F   On right, House of Julius.
- G   House of an Apothecary.
- H   House of Modestus, at the corner of an Alley leading into the great Street.
- I   Opposite House of a Thermopolite, or Seller of warm Drinks.
- K   A well-preserved group of Houses.
- L   Towers in the Wall of the City.
- M   Ramparts.
- N   House and Street, called—of the Vestals.
- O   A Triclinium.
- P   The Amphitheatre.
- Q   Carriage Road.

R Entrance to the Square, called the Soldiers' Quarters, that being imagined to have been its ancient destination, various pieces of armour having been found in the rooms around, as were also the skeletons of some chained prisoners.
S Open Court.
T Tower and Reservoir in an open area.
V Vestibule or School.
W Temple of Isis.
X Temple of Æsculapius.
Y Puteal.
Z Pen for Victims.
a Niche and Altar.
b Excavation of the Queen Caroline.
c Curia, &c.
d Basilica.
e Excavation of the General Championet.
f Modern Houses.
g Temple discovered in 1817.
h Heretofore called the Houses of the Dwarfs, from many paintings exhibiting short, deformed species of monsters, bearing some resemblance to the human shape, having been found upon the walls; but subsequent excavations have laid open an enclosed space, surrounded by a portico of columns, with a raised temple in the midst of the area.

ETYMOLOGY.

According to Solinus, the name of Pompeia is derived from ΠΟΜΠΗ, in allusion to the pomp with which Hercules celebrated his victories, while awaiting his fleet at the mouth of the Sarnus. The learned Bryant derives Pompeii from the Egyptian article pi, and omphi, an oracle. He observes that there were several places so called, none of which could have taken their names from Pompey the Great. In seeking the etymology of this word,[1] Sir William Drummond observes, with Bryant, that of the two pillars called Pompeian, one stands at the Pharos of Alexandria[2] in Egypt, the other at the eastern

[1] Herculanensia.
[2] Bryant, in support of his hypothesis, declares that the pedestal of the

point of the Thrasian Bosphorus—at a mouth of the Nile, and at the mouth of the Straits; whence he concludes that the name arose from the local situation; "pom" having the same signification in Chaldaic with "peh" in Hebrew, both meaning a mouth, edge, or extremity. The learned author therefore understands Pompeh to signify, the edge of the mouth, which he observes is precisely descriptive of the situation of this city with regard to the Sarnus.

The Etrurians, when in possession of nearly the whole of Italy,[1] and masters of Campania, founded there twelve cities; of which Capua, originally Vulturnum, the principal, afterwards became, both in power and the number of its inhabitants, the rival of Rome.[2] These cities appear generally to have sought security from piratical attack by situations retired from the shore.

The establishment of the Greeks on the shores of this part of Italy is one of the most certain facts recorded in ancient history, though the time of their coming is involved in obscurity. Œnotrus, according to Pausanias, was the first who led a colony hither about 1700 years before the vulgar æra.

Alexandrian pillar is older than the shaft. An inscription upon the former, according to Hamilton, (Ægyptiaca,) mentions the name of Diocletian. Dr. Clarke reads Hadrian.

[1] Strabo.
[2] Alteram Romam.—Cic. Phil. 12.

"... pelago cultuque penuque potentem
Deliciis, opibus famaque ...."
AUSONIUS.

Cumæ, the oldest city in Italy,[1] was originally a colony from Chalcis in Eubœa, and by means of the ships which conveyed its founders, became comparatively a considerable naval power; with its superabundant population was founded the neighbouring city Palæpolis, as also the adjoining Neapolis. These cities, in the year U. C. 428, considered themselves able to cope with the Roman power.[2]

To a state of which the political importance was principally derived from commerce, the mouth of the Sarnus would naturally present itself, as a point of considerable importance for ensuring commercial intercourse with the fertile plain south of Vesuvius, through which that river flowed.

That the coast opposite Caprea was held by Greeks, we learn from Tacitus,[3] who also informs us, that the Theleboi or Taphians, a piratical people [4] from the mouth of the Achelous, occupied that island. Virgil[5] expressly states, that having obtained possession of Caprea, they extended their dominion over the country in the vicinity of the Sarnus; to which, according to Conon as cited by Servius, they gave its name, and called their colony in its vicinity Sarrasti.

Thus the probability seems to be that Pompeii derived

---

[1] Strabo; and *vide* Athenæus. Livy, ix, 19, A. U. C. 425, speaks of all the coast, from Thurii to Cumæ, as possessed by Greeks.

[2] Livy, viii, 22.

[3] Ann. iv, 67. Græcos ea tenuisse, Capreasque Thelebois habitatas fama tradit.

[4] Τάφιοι, ληίστορες ἄνδρες. ΟΔ. Ο. 426.

[5] Æneid, vii, 735. See also Apollodorus, ii, 4; Pliny, iv, 12.

its origin from Greeks; a supposition strongly corroborated by the style of its architectural ornaments and buildings. Ought we not, therefore, to look to the language of that nation for the etymology of its name?

Palæpolis and Neapolis are so obviously Greek, that no learning has been brought forward to prove them otherwise; of the original name of the former we are ignorant, or whether it remained without any precise appellation until the foundation of the latter; but the names of both prove the continued use of the Greek language by their inhabitants.[1]

Pompaios was an epithet of Mercury, from the circumstance of his being the conductor of migrating souls[2] to the infernal regions. Πομπη is used by Homer to express a conductor.[3] May not the city of Pompeii have received its name from the same root, and have been called the Colony, as Naples was the new city?

---

[1] Nero, according to Tacitus, loved Naples for its Greek, of which the purity is spoken of by Philostratus 150 years after the first eruption of Vesuvius.

[2] "Tu pias, lætis animas reponis
  Sedibus. . . . ." Hor., lib. i, car. 10.

[3] ". . . . . . ὄφρα τάχιστα
Πομπῆς καὶ νόστοιο τύχῃς παρὰ πατρὸς ἐμεῖο."
         ΟΔ. Ζ. 289.

Plato, εκπομπη αποικων· the sent out, to found a colony. Πομποί· οἱ παραπέμποντες, ἢ προπομποί.—Scholiast. in Hom. Θ, 556—Γ.

Strabo calls Pompeii the επινειον, or emporium receiving and exporting εκπεμποντι, the merchandise of the neighbouring plain.

HISTORICAL NOTICE.

History, ever loving the marvellous, has delighted to shed over her early pages the obscurity of fiction, and, ranging beyond humanity, to dismiss from her memory every circumstance not calculated to excite our surprise. A race of heroes and gigantic chieftains, their daring enterprise and valorous exploit, in all the uncertainty of tradition, adorned with the graces and fictions of poetry, are first exhibited. Emerging from a state of barbarity, without inquiring whether they were the result of superior wisdom or unjudging caprice, nations have invariably shown that superstitious reverence for the institutions of their ancestors, which has led them to give implicit belief to any tale of their origin, however incredible, and to consider it more worthy of repetition, almost in an inverse ratio to its appearance of truth. Few indeed are the early notices of history which are not enveloped in the obscurities of fable; for it was not until she approached more civilised ages that we find her recitals governed by fact, or her narrations bearing the semblance of probability. Athens and Rome, founded by the immediate descendants of deities, in their subsequent greatness were worthy her contemplation; but it was scarcely until the former was mistress of art, that the passing events of her history were noticed; or until the latter had surpassed most other nations in her exertions for power, that she produced historians worthy to record them.

Campania, peopled by giants,[1] is fabled to have been visited by Hercules. It was held afterwards by the Osci, and their successors, the Etrurians or Pelasgi. The beauty of the country attracted, and the exuberance of its vines[2] allured, the arms of the neighbouring Samnites, who defended their possession with resolute courage, but were in turn obliged to submit to the increasing and less transient dominion of Rome.[3]

The battle of Cannæ delivered, but superinduced every calamity to the Campanians. The ferocity of Hannibal was mitigated by the submissive behaviour of the Capuans. They entered sincerely into the views of the Carthaginian, who declared their city should be the

[1] Diodorus Siculus.
[2] The famous Falernian wine was the produce of Campania.
[3] About 424 B.C.

future capital of Italy; but thirteen years of protracted warfare devastated their fields and exhausted their resources. Foiled in all his attempts, and unequal to the task of defending his conquests against the indefatigable valour and exertions of Rome, that general retiring his armies, abandoned the Capuans to their fate, and the unrelenting conqueror left the unpeopled walls a terrible example to those who meditated resistance to her encroachments.

The historian exultingly relates, that the majesty of Rome wreaked not its vengeance upon the unoffending walls and habitations; but he scruples not to say, that the scourged senators were butchered in a mass, and not an individual of the population escaped interminable slavery.

In all the minute detail of these operations, as related by Livy, mention is not made of either of the overwhelmed cities; although the possession of no town appears to have been considered sufficiently unimportant to remain undisputed. Hannibal marches from Nola to Naples, retraces his steps, and proceeds to the attack of Nuceria; but the interposition of Vesuvius seems to have afforded effectual security to this part of the coast.

The Social or Marsic war[1] proved equally calamitous to the conquered. Sylla, leading the legions of Rome,

---

[1] Began B.C. 91, by the Marsi, Peligni, Vestini, Marucini, and joined by the Picentes, Ferentani, Hirpini, Pompeiani, Venusini, Apuli, Lucani, and Samnites: their forces amounted to a hundred thousand.—APPIAN.

"Nec Annibalis nec Pyrrhi fuit tanta vastatio."
FLORUS.

soon put an end to the ephemeral success of this league. Stabia, though forced into the contest, was submitted to the unbridled license of a military mob. Villas, interspersed with the ruins of the devastated city,[1] thenceforth marked its site, affording melancholy evidence of the merciless policy of the Dictator. By what means Pompeii, a principal in the war, escaped a similar fate, we are not informed.[2]

Two circumstances alone, in the history of Pompeii, remain to be noticed:—a tumult which took place A.D. 59, within the walls; and an earthquake, which nearly destroyed it, four years after. Of the former Tacitus speaks:[3] "A disgraceful fray took place between the colonies Nuceria and Pompeii, at a show of gladiators given by Livineius Regulus, a degraded senator. From provincial sarcasms arose mutual reproaches; and from stones recourse was had to arms. The Pompeians, in whose city the spectacle was given, victorious, drove their adversaries out, but not without some slaughter: the wounded Nucerians went to Rome, and, deploring the loss of sons or fathers, appealed to the emperor for justice.

"Nero referred the affair to the senate: the senate, from the report of the consuls, decreed the prohibition of

---

[1] "Stabiam delevit."—PLINY.

[2] Sylla, at one time, had his camp on the Pompeian hill, (Plutarch, *in Vitâ*); and Paterculus says, that, in conjunction with Minatius Magius, he took the city. We find, too, that part of their lands were occupied by a colony, sent under the nephew of the dictator, to whom the Pompeians would not admit a right of ambulation in the porticoes or suffrage.

[3] Annales, xiv, 17.

such spectacles to the Pompeians for the space of ten years, and punished with exile Regulus, together with the most active in the tumult."

Tacitus also speaks of the earthquake.[1] Seneca[2] adds, that not only Pompeii, but Herculaneum, was nearly ruined, and that many other Campanian cities were more or less injured. Happening in February, a season of the year before supposed to have been exempt from such visitations, it seemed the forerunner of the great catastrophe which took place shortly afterwards, and the first interruption to the repose they had so long enjoyed, to have announced to the Pompeians the instability of their possessions. Filled with apprehension and alarm, they hesitated to repair its ravages; for the terror it inspired was so great, that many wandered about, deprived of their reasoning faculties; but, with continued tranquillity, confidence returned, and the restoration of their edifices was in great progress towards completion, when their final fate burst upon them. The workmen's tools are still, in many instances, found accompanying the materials collected for the repair of the damages this earthquake had caused.

Pompeii, although honoured by Seneca and Tacitus with the epithet of celebrated, was comparatively an insignificant city. Bearing but a small share in the ineffectual struggles of the country, its name[3] is scarcely

---

[1] Annales, xv, 22. "Opidum Pompeii magna ex parte proruit."

[2] Quæstiones, vi, 1.

[3] B.C. 308, Publius Cornelius lands at Pompeii, to ravage the fields of the Nucerians; which circumstance would seem to favour the idea of those

mentioned in the annals of its subjugators; and although the awful catastrophe which effected its ruin in the 1st century, has fortunately been the means of preservation in that ruin for the admiration as well as instruction of the 18th, and raised it in the estimation of the antiquary to equal in interest the more important cities of antiquity, yet, dignified only in its ultimate and singular destiny, its ruins alone are left to research. No historical record determines the precise period of the foundation, no existing document recounts any material event in its history; while, in the absence of all information as to the circumstances attending the rise, we turn to the magnificent engine of its fall, whose rugged summits, torn and reft by the force of a continued series of destructive fires, meet our view at the end of every street in its extent, and form a majestic back ground to every object it presents.

Nature[1] has indeed shed over the face of the surrounding country all her most enchanting beauties, yet not unmingled with her most awful terrors; and whether we look to its ancient traditionary story, as embellished by all the pleasing fictions of the poet, or contemplate

---

who consider it to have been a seaport. (See page 2; Livy, ix, 38.) Yet Hannibal, with his camp behind Tifata, when the great object of all his operations was to obtain possession of a harbour, never attacked it; which we may presume he would have done had it possessed that advantage, almost necessary to the existence of his army.

[1] "Omnium non modò Italia, sed toto orbe, terrarum pulcherrima Campaniæ plaga est: nil mollius cœlo: denique bis floribus vernat, nihil uberius solo: ideo Liberi Cererisque certamen dicitur. Hic amicti vitibus montes, et pulcherrimus omnium Vesuvius."—FLORUS.

the more instructive narrations of the historian; whether the intellect be refined and delighted with the charm of retrospect, or the eye wander over the endless varieties of its present surface; we find the scene equally enlivened by all the splendour of nature, and dignified by the finest productions of genius : it inspired the muse of Virgil, and afforded retirement to Cæsar.

> ". . Virgilium me . . . dulcis alebat
> Parthenope, studiis florentem ignobilis otî."

Torn by ever-recurring earthquake, with all the horrible phenomena of subterraneous convulsion, devastated by torrents of liquid fire, and overwhelmed by showers of boiling, stony mud; its cities suddenly swept from the face of the earth; that its inhabitants should still continue faithful to the soil, has excited the surprise of the philosopher. But let him turn to that region where all these terrors are increased tenfold by every rigour of the most frightful climate; where " beds of raging fire are only diversified by fields of starving ice," and inexhaustible fountains of boiling liquid; let him recollect, that at a time when barbarity had spread its dominion over degraded Europe, and shrouded it in a night of ignorance, literature there found a refuge, and, solaced by retrospect, could hope for the return of the light of science, though uncheered by the genial rays of a more southern sun.[1]

The destruction of the cities of Herculaneum, Pompeii,

---

[1] Every information with regard to the literature of Iceland may be found in Mackenzie's 'Voyage.'

and Stabia[1] took place, according to Pliny the Younger, who was an eye-witness of that catastrophe, August the 24th, in the second year of the reign of the emperor Titus, or A.D. 79.[2]

Frequent as have been the eruptions of Vesuvius since that which consigned these cities to a temporary oblivion, it appears to have shown no active indications of its volcanic nature for some centuries previously; for we find no memorial whatever of such an event, since historians had existed to record its phenomena.

The city of Pompeii itself, certainly of ancient date, is founded upon a stratum of lava, which stretches into the plain; though this, without having proceeded from Vesuvius, may have been at once produced, as in Iceland, where immense floods seem to have burst from vast rents in the earth, overwhelming the surrounding country to an incredible extent. Indeed, the whole exterior region of Vesuvius, as it now presents itself, appears to be founded upon this material, and to have been anciently a submarine Katakekaumene.[3] The lava near the sea is found twenty-five feet below its surface,[4] at the foot of the mountain, which, like all others of a similar description, may be looked upon as a vast accu-

---

[1] Stabia only existed as the site of some villas. "Sylla delevit quod nunc in villas abiit."—PLINY.

[2] Titus reigned from June, 78, to September, 80. From Cedrenus we learn, that the fire which happened at Rome, immediately after this eruption, was in the second year of his reign.

[3] The volcanic country of Asia Minor. (*Vide* Strabo.)

[4] Sir W. Hamilton.

mulation of volcanic matter around the orifice whence it has principally been ejected.

The first author who describes Vesuvius is Diodorus Siculus, who flourished forty-four years before the Christian æra. He says it then bore many corroborative marks of the truth of the tradition, of its having, like Ætna, burnt in remote times;[1] while Vitruvius, who appears to have little more than translated Diodorus, states, that the internal fires, which every where abounded in this part of Campania, had formerly increased under Vesuvius, until their superabundance had been ejected upon the surrounding country.

Strabo, A.D. 25, describes Vesuvius as clothed with a most fertile soil, except the nearly level top; this, exhibiting caverns and fissures, was totally sterile, being covered with stones, which appeared to have sustained the action of fire.[2] From these circumstances, he conjectures the mountain to have been originally volcanic, until deficiency of material occasioned its extinction.

Martial, in an epigram, written immediately after the first eruption, deplores the desolated state of Vesuvius, and describes it, before that event, to have been overshadowed by the most luxuriant vines and vegetation,— a retreat for which the gods of pleasure and gaiety

---

[1] Κατὰ τους αρχαιους χρόνους.

[2] It is presumed Strabo speaks of its external appearance, since we learn from other sources, that there was vegetation in the crater.

This geographer has been erroneously quoted as comparing Vesuvius to an amphitheatre,—a form, Dio says, it had assumed after the eruption of 79.

forsook their most favoured abodes;[1] and Tacitus, speaking of the residence of the emperor Tiberius, in the island of Capræa, extols the beauty of the view thence over the bay of Naples; for, as he observes, Vesuvius had not then changed the face of the country. Baiæ, Puteoli, Naples, Herculaneum, Pompeii, Surrentum, in an uninterrupted succession of towns and villas, seemed one continued city;[2] while the rugged walls of Vesuvius presented a natural fortress, towering above the whole, its sloping sides covered with the richest vines of Italy.

The circumstances attending the commencement of the Spartic war, clearly show that the appearance of the crater of Vesuvius at that period, B.C. 73, is nearly represented by the extinct volcano Astruni at the present time.[3]

The gladiator Spartacus, with seventy fellow-slaves, resolved upon the desperate attempt of breaking the bonds of slavery, to which, in its most cruel shape, he was subjected. With every advantage of situation,

[1] "Hic est pampineis viridis Vesuvius umbris:
Presserat hic madidos nobilis uva lacus.
Hæc juga, quam Nysæ colles, plus Bacchus amavit,
Hoc nuper Satyri monte dedere choros.
Hæc Veneris sedes, Lacedæmone gratior illi:
Hic locus Herculeo nomine clarus erat:
Cuncta jacent flammis et tristi mersa favillâ:
Nec vellent superi hoc licuisse sibi!"

[2] Strabo.

[3] This crater, near the Solfattara, about six miles in circumference, has but one entrance. The enclosed space is used as a royal park, and is stocked with wild animals. A crater completed from the scale of the Mount Somma would be about this extent.

Vesuvius presented itself to him, as an "altar on which he might place his hopes of freedom." Its summit, encompassed by an abrupt and rugged natural wall, contained an enclosed space, within which, with his adherents, soon augmented to ten thousand, he found a secure refuge. To this but one narrow and difficult passage afforded access. Hither being gradually driven, and closely invested by the prætor Clodius, who had been sent from Rome against him, he made ladders by twisting the branches of wild vines, which grew on the mountain, descended through the hollows between the ridges on the side where it was considered inaccessible, and consequently unwatched, fell upon the prætor unexpectedly with such vigour, that he defeated his troops and destroyed his camp.[1]

But, although the uncertain voice of tradition had reached the historian, the broken summits of Vesuvius had not attracted the notice of the poets. The latter, who have generally availed themselves of any doubt or ambiguity of the former, have left Vesuvius unembellished by a single beauty more than it presented, and unaccompanied by any of those terrors it was so well calculated to inspire.

Horace names it not; and Virgil, who attaches to every remarkable object in its vicinity some pleasing or tremendous recollection, only celebrates the soil of Vesuvius as remarkable for fertility:

---

[1] Plutarch, in Crassi Appian, Bell. Civ., i, 423; Livy, 97; Florus, iii, 20; Eutropius.

"Quæque suo viridi semper se gramine vestit,
Illa tibi lætis intexet vitibus ulmos
Illa ferax oleæ est . . . . .
Talem dives arat Capua et vicina Vesevo
Ora jugo."[1]   GEO., ii.

But neither Vesuvius nor Ætna appear to have been in a state of activity in the time of Homer, 900 years B.C., although the volcanic nature of the country seems not to have been unknown to him. Accordingly, we find an awful horror thrown over the whole coast. It is represented as the ultimate limit of the unfruitful ocean and habitable world. An impervious gloom, unenlivened by rising or setting sun, spread a thick, eternal shade over the beach, where the dark and barren groves of the remorseless Proserpine marked the entrance to the regions of the dead.[2]

But Ætna, Pindar, who lived from B.C. 521 to 435, describes in one of his finest passages, "νιφοεσσ' Αιτνα πανετες," &c.[3] He also celebrates the victory obtained by Gelon in the Crater or bay[4] of Naples, affording, perhaps, in both instances, a sort of negative proof with respect to the state of Vesuvius at that period, as he would probably have alluded to that mountain had

---

[1] Varro mentions its salubrious soil: "Ubi montana loca ut in Vesuvio, quod leviora et ideo salubriora." Also Polybius, and, in later times, Procopius, says, physicians sent their consumptive patients to it,—"tabe affectos."

[2] Iliad, K. L.

[3] The second recorded eruption of Ætna took place about 479, when the poet was forty-one. (Thucydides.)

[4] Pyth. Od., i, 139; and see Diod., 11, 51.

he been aware of any indications of the existence of its volcanic nature.

Of the eruption which destroyed Pompeii, a most satisfactory account is given by Pliny the Younger, in two letters written to Tacitus, with the intention of furnishing the historian with correct materials relative to that event.[1]

It appears that many and frequent shocks of earthquake had been felt for some days previously; but as these were phenomena by no means uncommon in Campania, extraordinary alarm was not excited by that circumstance,[2] until, about one o'clock in the afternoon of the 24th of August, a vast and singular cloud was seen to elevate itself in the atmosphere. From what mountain it proceeded was not readily discernible at Misenum,[3] where Pliny the Elder (at that time) held the command of the Roman fleet. This cloud continued arising in an uniform column of smoke, which varied in brightness, and was dark and spotted, as it was more or less impregnated with earth and cinders. Having

---

[1] It is singular that the learned author of the 'Classical Tour' should have imagined that the demolition of the palace of Portici, which is built over and prevents further excavations at Herculaneum, could be rewarded by the recovery of the lost books of Tacitus, the greater part of whose history treated of a period subsequent to the destruction of the cities.

[2] Other phenomena had also been remarked, although no inference had been drawn from their occurrence. Pliny, ii, 51, says, that a Pompeian decurion, Marcus Herennius, had, in a serene day, been struck dead by lightning.—" In Catilianis prodigiis Pompeiano ex municipio M. Herennius decurio sereno die fulmine ictus est." There is a house in the first street bearing the name Suettius Herennius.

[3] Fifteen miles distant.

attained an immense elevation, expanding itself, it spread out horizontally, in form like the branches of the pine, and precipitated the burning materials with which it was charged upon the many beautiful but ill-fated towns which stood thick upon this delightful coast.[1] The extraordinary phenomenon now excited the curiosity of Pliny, who ordered a vessel to be prepared, for the purpose of proceeding to a nearer inspection; but meeting some of the fugitives, and learning its destructive effects, his curiosity was changed to commiseration for the distressed, to whose succour he immediately hastened.

On approaching Retina, the cinders falling hotter as well as in greater quantity, mixed with pumice-stones, with black and broken pieces of burning rock; the retreat and agitation of the sea, driven backwards by the convulsive motion of the earth, together with the disrupted fragments hurled from the mountain on the shore, threatened destruction to anything which attempted to advance. Pliny therefore ordered the ship to be steered towards Stabia, where he found the alarm so great, that his friend Pomponianus had already conveyed his more portable property on board a vessel. The historian, less apprehensive, after partaking of a

---

[1] A similar mass, which issued from Vesuvius during the eruption of 1631, was estimated by the Abbe Braccini, it being measured with a quadrant, to exceed thirty miles in height. This computation must, however, be considered as erroneous; since Dr. Scotto, who saw it from Naples, says, the angle it subtended was thirty degrees, which would not give an elevation of five miles.

meal with his friend, went to bed; but was, however, soon obliged to remove, as, had he remained much longer, it was feared the falling cinders would have prevented the possibility of forcing a way out of the room. Still the town had not yet been materially affected, nor had the ravages of this great operation of nature reached Misenum; but suddenly broad refulgent expanses of fire burst from every part of Vesuvius, and, shining with redoubled splendour through the gloom of night, which had come on, glared over a scene, now accompanied by the increased horrors of a continued earthquake, which, shaking the edifices from their foundations, and precipitating their roofs upon the heads of the affrighted beings who had thought to find shelter in them, threatened universal desolation.

Driven from their homes, which no longer afforded security, the unfortunate inhabitants sought refuge in the fields and open places, covering their heads with pillows, to protect themselves from the increasing fall of stones and volcanic matter,[1] which accumulated in such quantity as to render it difficult to withdraw the feet from the mass, after remaining still some minutes; but the continuance of internal convulsion still persecuted

---

[1] In 1799, at Ottaiano, three miles distant from the crater, stones fell of 100 pounds weight, and the ashes were driven to Manfredonia in two hours, a distance of 100 miles.

The largest stones at Stabia do not much exceed an ounce, but many at Pompeii have been found to weigh eight pounds. Sir W. Hamilton observed, that some of the skulls found at the latter place had evidently been fractured.

them; their chariots,[1] agitated to and fro, even propped with stones, were not to be kept steady; while, although now day elsewhere, yet here most intense darkness was rendered more appalling by the fitful gleams of torches, at intervals obscured by the transient blaze of lightning.[2]

Multitudes now crowded towards the beach, as the sea, it was imagined, would afford certáin means of retreat; but the boisterous agitation of that element, alternately rolling on the shore and thrown back by the convulsive motion of the earth, leaving the marine animals upon the land it retreated from, precluded every possibility of escape.

At length, preceded by a strong sulphureous stench, a black and dreadful cloud, skirted on every side by forked lightning, burst into a train of fire and igneous vapour, descended over the surface of the ocean, and covered the whole bay of the crater,[3] from the island of Capreæ,[4] to the promontory of Misenum with its noxious exhalations; while the thick smoke, accompanied by a

---

[1] Sir W. Hamilton remarks, that, in 1794, the gentry of Naples, fearing the effects of the eruption, slept in the open places in their chariots.

[2] Pliny does not notice the accompanying noise: this must have materially increased the horror of the scene. Sir W. Hamilton describes it as a mixture of the loudest thunder, combined with never-ceasing reports as from the heaviest artillery, accompanied by a continued hollow murmur, like the sea during a violent storm, and the rushing noise of an ascent of rockets. Nor does he remark the torrents of water and glutinous mud which form strata at Pompeii. Zonaras describes the former as like the collision of mountains falling together; but modern science has invented new objects for simile.

[3] The Bay of Naples was anciently called the Bay of the Crater.

[4] Distant twenty-two miles.

slighter shower of ashes, rolled like a torrent among the miserable and affrighted fugitives; who, in the utmost consternation, increased their danger by pressing forward in crowds, without an object, amidst darkness and desolation:[1] now were heard the shrieks of women, screams of children, clamours of men, all accusing their fate, and imploring death, the deliverance they feared, with outstretched hands to the gods, whom many thought about to be involved, together with themselves, in the last eternal night.

Three days and nights were thus endured in all the anguish of suspense and uncertainty; many were doubtless stifled by the mephitic vapour;[2] others, spent with the toil of forcing their way through deep and almost impassable roads, sunk down to rise no more; while those who escaped, spread the alarm, with all the circumstances of aggravation and horror which their imaginations, under the influence of fear, suggested. At length a gleam of light appeared, not of day, but fire; which, passing, was succeeded by an intense darkness, with so heavy a shower of ashes, that it became necessary to keep the feet in motion, to avoid being

---

[1] This torrent of smoke proved fatal, at Stabia, to the Elder Pliny, who was there suffocated on the sea-beach. And this was probably the fate of all who, fatigued, lay down, and thereby put themselves within the influence of the mofete. Lanterns have been sometimes found with the bodies.
the eruption, 1631, a similar cloud was estimated to cover 100 square miles of country: men and beasts were struck dead by the electric fluid which issued therefrom during its progress.

[2] The mofete sometimes interrupts the progress of the excavations at Pompeii: where it is prevalent, the vines will not grow.

fixed and buried by the accumulation. On the fourth day the darkness by degrees began to clear away, the real day appeared, the sun shining forth sickly as in an eclipse; but all nature, to the weakened eyes, seemed changed; for towns and fields had disappeared under one expanse of white ashes, or were doubtfully marked, like the more prominent objects after an alpine fall of snow.

If such be the description of this most tremendous visitation, as it affected Stabia and Misenum, comparatively distant from the source of the calamity, what must have been the situation of the unfortunate inhabitants of Pompeii, so near, of Herculaneum within, its focus? Must we not conclude that, at the latter place at least, most of those not overwhelmed by the torrents of stony mud[1] which preceded others of flaming lava, burying their city sixty feet under the new surface,[2] were overtaken by the showers of volcanic matter in the fields, or drowned in attempting to escape by sea, their last but hopeless resource, since it appears to have received them to scarcely less certain destruction?

The emperor Titus, whose great and good qualities here found every opportunity for their display, immediately hastened to this scene of affliction; appointed curatores,[3]

---

[1] The lower stratum at Herculaneum appears to be a species of tufa, deposited in a fluent state.

[2] Herculaneum is at present, in some parts, buried one hundred and twelve feet below the surface.

[3] Suetonius *in Vitâ*.

persons of consular dignity, to set up the ruined buildings, and take charge of the effects of those who perished without heirs, for the benefit of the surviving sufferers; to whom he remitted all taxes, and afforded that relief the nature of their circumstances required; personally encouraging the desponding, and alleviating the miseries of the sufferers, until a calamity of an equally melancholy description recalled him to the capital, where a most destructive fire, laying waste nearly half the city, and raging three days without intermission, was succeeded by a pestilence, which for some time carried off ten thousand persons daily.

The eruptions after that of Titus appear to have been of very frequent recurrence; but the first of consequence occurred under Severus about the year 200. The accompanying noise was heard as far as Capua. Dion Cassius informs us, that the summit of the mountain had then assumed the form of an immense amphitheatre, of which the present Monte di Somma formed the north-eastern half or wall; the rest having been thrown down at some later period, subsequent to which the now highest top containing the crater was formed.

After 305,[1] Diocletian.—The violence of the eruption which occurred in the reign of the emperor Leo[2] next

---

[1] This eruption is doubtful, and was probably invented for the purpose of introducing St. Januarius, who, about this time, was put to death in the amphitheatre of Nola.
Nonnus, in the 4th century, calls Vesuvius three-topped.

[2] Olybrius held the Western Empire.

attracted the notice of the historians.[1] The internal fermentation and unceasing convulsion which shook the mountain, accompanied by a series of tremendous explosions during the years 471, 472, 473, spread devastation over the adjacent country, and alarm throughout the rest of Europe, the surface of which was covered with an impalpable powder.[2] At Constantinople the falling cinders, at one time, struck such panic terror into the superstitious mind of the pusillanimous emperor, that, leaving the city, which he deemed devoted to divine wrath, he betook himself to St. Mamas;[3] and the day was ordained to be for ever annually marked by supplication. St. Januarius[4] was supposed on this occasion to have quelled the fury of the volcano, it being the first time he is said to have appeared.

Under Theodoric, 512, we find the destructive effects to have been so severe, that the taxes were remitted to the people of Campania.[5] The exhalation alone was so thick[6]

---

[1] Marcellinus.—Procopius de Bell. Got., lib. ii.

[2] An impalpable powder of this description fell in rain during a procession of St. Nicholas, February, 1813, when the writer was at Zante. It tinged linen on which it fell of an ochreous yellow. After the shower, the deposition lay on the decks of the ships in the bay in considerable quantity.

[3] Sigonius, Imp. Occident., lib. xiv. In a separated quarter of the city there were a church, palace, bridge, and hippodrome of St. Mamas. In the latter, one Andreas was whipped to death by order of the pious emperor Constantine Iconomachus, for excelling in the art of sculpture.

[4] Baronius.

[5] Cassiodorus, lib. iv, epist. 50.

[6] Sigonius.

and black, as to involve the country in darkness, while the noise and continued tremor excited universal terror. The cinders covered the transmarine provinces; clouds of sandy dust and fine ashes, poured with the force and impetus of mighty torrents, overwhelming the country to the tops of the trees, and every where converting the verdure of nature into the dreary aridity of the desert.

In 556, Justinian the Great.—The mountain uttered terrifying sounds, to the great alarm of the people; but no eruption took place.[1]

685 or 686.—The country for thirty miles round was shaken by earthquake, and the explosions were attended by vast torrents of lava; while the city of Naples was supposed to have been saved by the interposition of St. Januarius, who, active in quelling its fury, was imagined in the air over the volcano, by the superstitious, in whose minds it also foretold the dissolution of Pope Benedict II.

993, 1036, 1049.[2]—The explosions of Vesuvius were, during these ages, no longer looked upon as great operations of nature. They were only regarded as the pranks of those supernatural beings, whose sole power over humanity was the infliction of evil; the boundaries of hell were here supposed to be advanced amongst the abodes of the living, and the infernal fire exhibited upon earth, in terror to its degenerate inha-

---

[1] Procopius.
[2] Cronico Cassinense.

bitants; who were hurried into the abyss prepared for them, almost while life yet lingered over the remains of mortality.

An engine so well adapted to the purposes of priestcraft could hardly have escaped its professors. Accordingly we find an account written A.D. 1062, by B. Pietro Damiani, in Castigliano, which, although little illustrative of the history of Vesuvius, is curious as marking the age to which it was addressed; and affords better evidence of the continued activity of the volcano than can be drawn from the imperfect testimonials of the historians of the age. He relates that—

In the neighbourhood of the mountain dwelt a most devout hermit; who, one evening seeing upon the road a quantity of black men, apparently negroes, driving in haste before them a great number of mules loaded with fuel, accosted them, expressing his surprise at the singularity of their appearance. He was answered, that they were all devils, that the fuel was to burn the prince of Capua, who was then ill; and they added that Don Juan, constable of Naples, although in good health, if they were not mistaken, would soon be in their power also.

The holy man, giving up the cause of the prince as hopeless, immediately betook himself to the constable; told him all he had seen and heard, and exhorted him, as the only way of avoiding this disagreeable alternative, to become a monk. To this Don Juan was easily persuaded, since upon inquiry he found that in the interim the prince had expired: but, as he had received orders to join the emperor Otho, who was expected in a fortnight, for the purpose of driving the Saracens from Calabria, he deferred the execution of his pious resolution until the infidels were conquered: the consequence was, that he died before the emperor arrived; and we are assured, that at the moment of his decease Vesuvius burst forth into most dreadful flames, bellowing from a mouth whence fire everlastingly issues; which fire, it is added, always flamed with proportionate vehemence, pouring out rivers of rosin and brimstone whenever any rich and consequently wicked man died.

Damiani also considered it the receptacle of some souls not doomed to eternal damnation; for he states, that he himself knew a man who was not only in orders, and a priest, but also chaplain to a dignified prelate, who leaving his mother infirm at Beneventum, was proceeding towards Naples, when he saw Vesuvius shoot forth a great body of flames; while from the midst proceeded a sad and doleful voice, which he knew to be that of his mother. He noted the time, and afterwards found it to agree with the very moment at which she had expired.

An eruption in 1138 lasted forty days, and, assisted by a slighter one of the following year, seems to have exhausted the energies of Vesuvius, since we find it from that date remaining in a state of comparative inactivity for nearly five centuries.

Ambrosius Nolanus relates an account of an eruption about 1500, and mentions having heard of another seventy years before. In the 'Annals of Italy' we find one during the pontificate of Benedict IX: but the notices respecting these are uncertain. Meanwhile the neighbouring volcanoes were not inactive. The last eruption of Solfatara was in the year 1198; Ischia ceased 1302; and the Monte Nuovo, three miles in circumference, formed in forty-eight hours, 1538; while in the interim Ætna had sixteen explosions.

But the accounts we have from those who saw the crater of Vesuvius at the beginning of the 17th century, clearly lead to the conclusion, that this volcano must have remained in a comparative state of inactivity for a considerable period.

Pighi, during the pontificate of Sixtus V, compares the then existing crater to an immense amphitheatre, the arena of which seemed sunk to the bowels of the earth; the top surrounded by a vast bank of calcined stones, the sloping sides clothed with all sorts of trees,[1] amongst which wild animals sought shelter; for wherever the sun could penetrate, vegetation to a certain extent existed, except on one side, which was perpendicular and bare. By a winding way he descended, he thinks, nearly a mile, until the precipitous nature of the place and obscurity rendered further progress extremely hazardous: huge masses of volcanic matter and disrupted rock, obstructed in their descent by large trees,[2] torn up by their roots, contracted the space below; but

---

[1] The space or winding valley between the two summits, called the Atrio di Cavallo, also afforded pasture, and in it were pools of water. It is now a scene of perfect desolation.

[2] These rather countenance the account of the eruption of 1500. It was perhaps slight.

within he observed no signs of the volcano being in an active state, although, near the summit, on inserting the hand in the fissures, a slight heat was perceptible.

Braccini, who saw the mountain 1612, informs us, that the space between the two tops, called the Atrium, was then covered with vegetation, and afforded pasture. He computes the depth to which he descended, in the interior of the crater, to have been a mile. He was told that it was possible to descend two miles, and that, at the bottom, was a plain space, set round with caverns, so dark that no one had ventured to proceed within them.

In 1619, Magliocco found a way down the sides of the crater, which, continually narrowing, was at length obstructed by a large fragment of rock. This, with the steepness of the place, obliged him to go on hands and feet; thus passing it, the ruggedness of the rocky, projecting sides afforded him means of proceeding, until he arrived at the bottom, where, in the obscurity, he found a level space. In the midst of this was a huge mass of rock,[1] which seems to have covered the opening to the abyss, as from the fissures around its base issued a cold and vehement current of air.[2] He also observed three small pools of water, one of which was hot and

[1] Many masses of rock now lie around the base of the cone; one measures 19 feet in height by 66 in circumference; a second girts 100 feet, and is 17 high.

[2] The coldness of this current of air does not prove the fires of the volcano to have been extinct; for its passage through prolonged and contracted fissures would totally extract whatever degree of heat it might have acquired when passing over the surface of fire.

corrosively bitter, a second extremely salt, while the insipidity of the third he compares to chicken-broth without salt; it was of a high degree of temperature.[1]

Braccini gives a detailed account of the tremendous rebursting forth of Vesuvius, 1631; which appears what might have been expected after five centuries of comparative repose. From that period, the more authenticated history of the volcano may be said to commence. Thenceforward we find it seldom remaining more than ten years without an eruption. In the year 1764, Sir William Hamilton arrived at Naples, and Vesuvius obtained an observer who has given every and most satisfactory information respecting its phenomena. It only remains to the more extended observation of modern science, to mark a few singularities in its geological formation.

The history of Vesuvius has been followed to a greater extent than necessary to elucidate the subject of the excavated city; but it has been presumed, that some acquaintance with an object, of which the first phenomena were so fatal to Pompeii, would not be unacceptable. Sir William Hamilton's excellent accounts bring us nearly to the present day. From him we learn, that the lava does not always issue from the crater; in 1766, it burst forth from a spot half a mile lower down, the adjacent ground quivering like the timbers of a windmill. The inflamed matter was so intensely hot at the source, as to prevent a nearer

---

[1] Astruni contains wild boars, and has three pools.

approach than ten feet; yet its toughness was such, that a stone of considerable magnitude, when thrown upon its surface, made but a slight impression, and was borne on by the current. Sometimes it issues like glass in fusion; at others, assumes a more farinaceous appearance, and comes out as meal from the grindstone; but its rapidity soon abates, and the extended surface becomes more sluggish, and is spotted with detached, cooling portions, which increase until the whole at length becomes a mere heap of stones, resembling a ploughed field or boisterous sea arrested by a sudden frost. On cooling, which is an operation of years, it cracks occasionally with loud explosion.[1]

The crater, as well as its internal opening, assumes various forms, and is acted upon by the casualties of the respective eruptions. In 1766, we find the inside containing a small plain or crust, from the midst of which arose a smaller cone. Of this, the apex, gradually increasing, at length became 200 feet higher than the outer rim. The intermediate hollow was afterwards filled with the overflowing lava of succeeding eruptions; so that, in 1779, we find the whole strengthened sufficiently to contain that material in fusion, which, suddenly ejected with violence and descending upon its sides, added much to the strength of the boundary.

The explosion of 1794 was attended by the not un-

---

[1] Sir William Hamilton, three years after the eruption of 1767, fired a stick by thrusting it within one of the crevices.

usual, on such occasions, scarcity of water in the wells and fountains, slight puffs of smoke issuing from the ground; and subsequently the extensive internal fermentation, which affected the neighbouring country as far as Beneventum, thirty miles distant, and even extended to Puglia. Fountains or jets of flame marked the commencement of the explosion, and, issuing from a long rent in the side of the mountain, threw balls of fire in all directions. Volleys of thunder, with darkness and agitation, succeeded. At Naples, for several hours, everything was in constant tremor; doors and windows swinging on their hinges, and bells incessantly ringing. At length, six hours after the commencement, the lava, finding vent, calmed the internal fever.

Innumerable had heretofore been the miracles worked by the exposition of sainted relics, and marvellous had been the interposition of their influence in other parts during this occasion. But in vain to the terror-stricken inhabitants of Torre del Greco was the head of the patron saint brought forth in procession. In vain did the Archbishop oppose his unliquefying blood to the fury of Vesuvius. The fiery torrent, uninfluenced by his presence, rolled on its course to the sea, laying waste and burying their town in its accumulation; but, of a population of 18,000, fifteen individuals only are supposed to have perished,[1] the mass having with difficulty

---

[1] Many escaped next day over the scoriæ upon the surface of the burning lava; and thus did a firework-maker save his stock in trade and gunpowder, his house having been surrounded, but not entered, by the lava.

saved their lives, obliged to abandon all their goods and effects. Torre del Greco is, perhaps, reserved for the research of the curious. After another interval shall have elapsed, its images may be again brought forth, and another museum may be formed of its remains, when those of Portici and Naples shall exist only in the pages of the antiquary.

PUBLIC WAYS.—TOMBS.

The Public Ways ranked amongst the most important of the works of Roman magnificence. Amazing labour, with vast expense, were devoted and combined in extending them from the Capitol to the utmost limits of the known world; and in many instances they seem to have been calculated by their construction to outlast the empire, of which they have, not inaptly, been termed the arteries.

Nor was their construction alone the object of solicitude; the care of looking to their repair was not thought unworthy of the greatest men of the republic. None but those of the highest rank were eligible to the office of superintending that service, and we find Augustus himself taking the charge of a district.

The Appian Way, the most ancient as well as most noble, being distinguished by the epithet of *Regina Viarum*, as originally made by Appius Claudius the Censor, extended from Rome to Capua.[1] It was composed of three strata; the lower, of rough stones or flint cemented together, formed a foundation or statumen; the middle stratum or rudera was of gravel; the upper of well-jointed stones of irregular forms. It remains in many places perfect to the present day.

From the Appian Way at Sinuessa, that afterwards called the Domitian branched off to Puteoli and Baiæ; while other ramifications continued along the coast through Herculaneum to Pompeii, where the Sarnus was crossed by a bridge, from which the road, immediately dividing, might be pursued to Stabia or Nocera.

Pompeii might also be approached from the other side of Vesuvius through Nola by the Popilian Way, which ran through that city to Reggio.[2]

These ways, conducting through a country naturally enriched by all the varieties of nature, were further

[1] Livy, ix, 29. Procopius, at the distance of nearly a thousand years, mentions it as still entire.

[2] Notwithstanding the excellence of their roads, the Romans travelled at best but slowly. Augustus took two days to go from Rome to Præneste, twenty-five miles. Horace, in his journey to Brundusium, takes the same time to go forty-three miles; but he thinks an expeditious traveller might do it in one day. There are, however, instances of extraordinary speed.

embellished with the most beautiful objects of art. Temples, ædiculæ, triumphal arches, sepulchres, villas, groves, gardens, were thrown together in the most picturesque irregularity; porticoes afforded shade, and inns shelter, refreshment, or repose to the traveller; who beheld, as he approached, the increasing capital thus stretched out in beautiful and endless suburbs;[1] for the Romans, in this prosperous age, were very far from entertaining a suspicion that it could ever become necessary to surround the seat of empire with walls.

The sepulchres occupying the sides of the public ways of course varied in magnificence, according to the taste or spirit and affluence of the patron; by whom they were considered as the last home after this life; the only property which did not descend to, and was not liable to be squandered by, the extravagant heir. Their beauty and interest were increased, not more from the taste or want of it, displayed in the architectural decoration and the picturesque groups they combined, than from the inscriptions they presented, which were oftentimes as instructive as the style and diction were varying. If the traveller obeyed their invitation, *siste viator*, he might pause to smile at the last lingering of human vanity, or contemplate the scanty notices of those who had successively contributed, by their courage and talents, to support in difficulty the state, or enlarge the empire until

---

[1] "Exspatiantibus tectis multas additas urbes."
PLINY, H. N.

its limits were unknown. Indignation might be excited at the sumptuous monument of the barber of Augustus or freedman of Claudius, while Pompey or Cato had little or no memorial to mark the place where their mortal remains were deposited.

> "Marmoreo Licinus tumulo jacet at Cato parvo;
> Pompeius nullo. Credimus esse Deos?"
>
> MART.

But the philosopher could content himself in the reflection, that, however birth or fortune might vary the lot of the living, time would ultimately put a period to all distinction; since even marble could not ensure immortality.

> "Miremur periisse homines? monumenta fatiscunt.
> Mors etiam saxis nominibusque venit:
> . . . . sunt fata Deûm, sunt fata locorum."[1]

Mausolea were sometimes erected, the expense of which, as in the instance of Mausolus, impoverished the state which reared them; but this was reckoned amongst the wonders of the ancient world. Not less splendid were those of Porsenna at Clusium; of Augustus, surmounted by his statue in bronze; or that of Hadrian; each of which might have been considered an additional marvel, had not buildings of such magnitude ceased to be rare at Rome, for the embellishment of which capital they were reserved.

[1] Ausonius—Statius.

The sepulchral monuments of the ancients are certainly to be sought for without the entrances to their cities; for although the very illustrious were sometimes honoured, by public decree, with sepulture in the forum and public places within the walls, yet this was a distinction but rarely conferred, and by some cities never allowed. In the early ages of society, indeed, a different practice appears to have prevailed; for the constant apprehension of attack under which the smaller states must have existed, would naturally prevent their exposing the remains of those most beloved in life, to the possibility of indignity from a victorious and generally remorseless enemy.

Thus we find an ancient law of the Thebans ordained that no man should build a house, without therein providing a proper burial-place for the family; and a similar custom was observed among the early Romans, whose dead were deposited within their dwellings,[1] until the law of the twelve tables forbade any corpse being either interred or burnt within the city.[2] That this ordinance was not strictly complied with, may be inferred from the frequency of its renewal.

Two motives have been imagined for the enactment of this law; pollution was thus avoided, and a great source of infection removed.[3] It might also have been ob-

---

[1] "Doliis aut vasculis:" in a species of receptacle, of a triangular prismatic shape, formed of three large rectangular tiles, with two triangular, closing the ends.

[2] "Hominem mortuum in urbe ne sepelito neve urito."—CIC.

[3] Isid. xiv, orig. 11.

served, that the old practice afforded considerable security against the detection of private murder.

To the same causes, as well as protection from violation, we may refer the custom of burning the dead.[1] The Egyptians, less apprehensive of an enemy, took, on the contrary, the greatest care to preserve the remains of mortality; and the Lacedæmonians, whose every law breathed defiance and contempt of their neighbours, and whose every institution was formed for the purpose of inspiring attachment to their homes, do not appear to have adopted this practice. They were ordered by Lycurgus to bury within the city.[2]

The veneration with which the ancients viewed their places of sepulture, seems to have formed the foundation upon which was raised their boundless mythology, and in some probability introduced the belief in national and tutelary gods, as well as the practice of worshipping them through the medium of statues: for the places where their heroes were interred, when ascertained, were held especially sacred,[3] and frequently a temple erected over their tomb hallowed the spot. It was thus the bodies of their fathers, buried at the entrance to the house, consecrated the vestibule to their memory,[4] and

---

[1] The custom of burning the dead seems to have fallen into disuse in the time of Macrobius, 4th century.

[2] This was also the custom of the Tarentines, in conformity with the response of an oracle, which pronounced that their city would flourish in proportion to the number of inhabitants it should contain.

[3] "Ubi corpus demortui hominis condas, locus sacer esto."—Cic.

[4] The statues or likenesses of a man's ancestors were placed in the

gave birth to a host of local deities, who, never forsaking, were supposed to hold that part of the dwelling under their peculiar protection.

Removed from the dwelling-houses to the highways, the tombs of the departed were still regarded as objects of the highest veneration. Every honour was rendered, and respect observed, which could tend to hallow them in the eyes of the living: while the strictest laws were instituted against the violators of their sanctity, whom the avenging goddess was supposed to pursue even beyond the grave.[1]

But some families still had burial-places at their country-houses; not choosing to have their names exhibited to the popular gaze, or their memory recalled to animadversion.[2]

And thus Propertius:

> "Dii faciant, mea ne terra locet ossa frequenti,
> Qua facit assiduo tramite vulgus iter.
> Post mortem tumuli sic infamantur amantum,
> . . . .
> Non juvat in media nomen habere via."

while it appears to have afforded a peculiar prospect of gratification to others, that each passer-by should wish them farewell.

---

vestibule; where, also, the corpse of the defunct was laid out on a couch, the feet towards the gate.—GELL., xvi, 5.

[1] Nemesis was thought to have especial care for the honour of the dead.

[2] Gruter.

T. LOLLIUS
HIC · PROPTER · VIAM · POSITUS
UT · DICANT · PRAETEREUNTES
LOLLI · VALE

But it seems to have required the continual infliction of penalties to restrain the rich, whose vanity constantly prompted them to infringe the sumptuary laws, both in the length of their epitaphs and the cost of their monuments, which were usually decorated with marble or highly ornamented and expensive stucco-work, with relievos sometimes painted, alluding to the profession or habits of the deceased, or subjects expressed in farfetched allegory.

Low relievos in stucco seem to have been used by the ancients very frequently, to give effect to those paintings which were intended to be left open to the air; as may be observed in many instances at Pompeii, where the tomb of Scaurus presents a prominent specimen. Modern painters would entertain but a mean opinion of the talents of those who could resort to this expedient to give relief to their representations; nor would sculpture now be deemed to receive improvement from the assistance of the sister art: yet we find Parrhasius[1] painting the work of Mys on the shield of the brazen Minerva of the Acropolis of Athens; and the brother of Phidias, according to Pliny,[2] was employed in a similar work at Elis.

---

[1] Pausanius Attic. 28.
[2] H. N. xxxv, 8.

Tombs, in various parts of Asia Minor, observed by the writer have been thus embellished. Upon a sky-blue ground figures sculpt in very flat relief, were covered with minium:[1] indeed most low reliefs, not excepting those done under the eye of Phidias in the Athenian Acropolis, were so finished, if not formed, for that express purpose.

Petronius may be referred to for some idea of the general intention in these representations upon the sepulchres of the ancients. The structure being raised, Trimalchio desires that the likeness of his dog may be formed at the feet of his statue, and the monument be adorned with garlands and representations of the combats which would take place at his funeral, as by such means he trusted his memory would survive. That the enclosure should extend a hundred feet in front and two hundred in depth, trees of different species being planted to form a grove within, around his remains; since he held it to be a mistaken idea, that those dwellings which could but be temporary should be alone worthy of care, while these, which were to be inhabited for ever, were to be neglected. He provides against any indignity being offered, or nuisance committed, by leaving to one of his freed-men the care of watching the depository of his remains;[2] and would have particularly expressed, that it descended not to his heir.

Upon the monument was to be carved a ship under

---

[1] And see Pausanias Achaic. 26.

[2] "Ne in monumentum populus cacatum currat."

full sail, with himself represented sitting on the deck, clothed in magisterial robes and insignia, pouring out riches upon the multitude; also a triclinium, and the people feasting therein.

At his right hand was to be placed the statue of his wife, with a dove, and holding a dog by a chain; around him well secured amphoræ, while one was to appear broken, and upon it a boy weeping the misfortune: the whole to be surmounted by a sun-dial; that the eye of the traveller might be attracted towards the inscription recording his name, modesty, riches, and good fortune, together with any thing else in his praise his heirs might think proper to add.

Frequently there were placed, at or within the sepulchre, the statues of the relatives or particular friends of the deceased; and thus the bust of the poet Ennius is mentioned by Livy to have occupied a place in the tomb of the Scipios.

We are informed by Cicero, that enclosed places for burial were prepared for the poor and slaves at the public expense,[1] although private munificence sometimes bequeathed land for that purpose.

We may learn also from the same authority, that the

---

[1] "Hoc miseræ plebi stabat commune sepulchrum."
Hor., Sat. I, viii, 10.

And here the dead bodies of malefactors were thrown:

"Post insepulta membra different lupi
Et Esquilinæ alites."
Hor., Epod. v, 99.

cost of burial-places in general was partly met by the public; and thus we may presume the sepulchral triclinium at Pompeii to have been formed, for the accommodation of those friends and relatives who might be inclined to do the customary honours to the memory of the deceased. Here a repast was provided, at which his merits were discussed, and his departure lamented. The party were dressed in white, the tomb adorned with flowers,[1] amongst which the rose was frequent.[2] Although wine was drunk, the repast was frugal: an edict of Numa forbade fish not having scales, lest the cost should be thereby increased: merriment was abstained from, being considered indecorous, where the intention was the solace of the friends, gratitude to and memory of the deceased, as well as propitiatory to the infernal deities.[3]

A provision was sometimes made by will for defraying the expenses of this celebration; as we learn from an inscription upon a monument found at Ravenna, wherein is stipulated that it should take place annually, the tomb being adorned with roses. On another at Rome, a similar observance and ceremony is enjoined, with a

---

[1] "Atque aliquis senior veteres veneratus amores
Annua constructo serta dabit tumulo."
TIBULLUS.

[2] Τοδε και νεκροις αμυνει.
ANACREON.

[3] Suetonius says, pantomimics were introduced, who imitated the manners of the deceased.

sacrifice to Pluto, Proserpine, and the infernal gods; the remains to be eaten by the company. The disappointed heir was apt to neglect this ceremony.[1]

To the custom of honouring excellence even after life, the historian Polybius refers, in a great measure, the cause of the higher qualities and superiority of the Romans over their enemies; for, says he, "this public institution excites the emulation of the rising as well as existing generation. When a man whose life has been worthy of imitation departs this world, his remains are still respected; and amongst the honours rendered, his corpse borne to the forum is there placed at the rostrum, so that it may be conspicuous, when the surrounding multitude are addressed by his son or nearest relative, who, ascending the rostrum, panegyrises his good qualities, and enumerates the various exploits he has done to the advancement of the interests or glory of his country; the memorable actions of his life are extolled, events in which, most probably, many present have borne a more or less distinguished share, or taken a particular interest; thus the praise bestowed upon the deceased becomes identified with their own, their finest feelings are awakened, and the loss of an individual becomes a source of public sorrow and sympathy.

"With the accustomed ceremonies consigned to the tomb, he is not forgotten; his enshrined image, the features and even complexion most accurately expressed,

[1] Catullus.

is placed in some conspicuous part of the dwelling he inhabited; on solemn occasions it is adorned and disclosed. When any of his posterity, after rendering themselves eminent, close the last scene of life, these busts are again brought forth; and, that the representation may be in all respects complete, clothed in the embroidered robes of the several dignities they had attained, and preceded by the appropriate insignia of the various offices they had respectively held, are in chariots drawn in the solemn procession. Arrived at the forum, the same curule chairs receive them with which when alive they were privileged. The orator, when the exhausted virtues of the recently deceased no longer afford him subject for eulogy, turns to those whose venerable likenesses recall to his imagination the celebrated deeds and various exploits they had performed, and which led to the honours by which they had been distinguished: he shows that, animated by the example of his predecessors, each in succession proved himself not unworthy his ancestors; and thus in the minds of their descendants infuses the hope of obtaining honorable fame, by the performance of every great and worthy action; for what spectacle can be more imposing, and who can without emotion behold the living, breathing likenesses[1] of those

---

[1] To modern feelings it is difficult to conceive other than ludicrous effects from the display of a wax-work ancestry; yet we have the testimony of more than one ancient to the good result of such exhibition:

"Sæpe audivi, Q. Maximum, P. Scipionem, præterea civitatis nostræ præclaros viros, solitos dicere; cum majorum imagines intuerentur, vehementissime accendi."—SALL., Bel. Jug.

whose prudence and skill, in the ardour of victory, only sought opportunity for magnanimity, and whose courage, undeterred by adverse fortune in the ignominy of defeat, only found new occasion for its display?"

STREET OF THE TOMBS.

Approaching Pompeii from Naples, both sides of the road, for nearly a furlong before entering the city, are occupied by tombs and public monuments, intermixed with shops; and in front of the latter, arcades were constructed, affording shelter from the rays of the sun or inclemency of the weather. The carriage way, or *agger*, exhibiting the tracks or ruts[1] worn by chariots, is narrow,

---

[1] These ruts are sometimes four inches deep; the wheels seem to have been about three inches wide, and from three feet to three feet six inches apart. The wheels of a modern carriage are about four feet six inches asunder.

seldom exceeding fourteen feet in width,[1] with footways or *margines* on each side, varying from four to six, elevated above the road about a foot, and separated therefrom by a curb[2] and guard stones, raised about sixteen inches, and placed at intervals of from ten to twelve feet asunder. The whole of the road is formed of lava in irregular shaped blocks, from ten to fourteen inches thick, originally well jointed and put together: indeed its state of preservation sufficiently attests the perfection of the principle upon which it was constructed. This,[3] although the principal entrance to the city, is not striking for its beauty, and is small in its dimensions. The walls of brick and rubble work are faced with stucco, which is covered with nearly illegible inscriptions of ordinances, &c. The centre archway is in width about fourteen feet seven inches, and might possibly have been twenty high; but its arch does not remain: it therefore in size scarcely equals that entrance to the city of London called Temple Bar. On each side were smaller openings for foot passengers, four feet six inches wide, their height being about ten. The road rises considerably into the city.

On the left, before entering the gate, is a pedestal, which appears to have been placed for the purpose of sustaining a colossal statue of bronze, some fragments of its drapery having been there found: this possibly was

[1] The great street, immediately within the gate, is about 21 feet; including the footways, 33 feet.

[2] In the curb-stone frequently occur holes for passing the halter.

[3] See Plate 19.

the tutelary deity of the city. On the opposite side is an arched recess, around and without which seats are formed; in the centre was an altar or pedestal. This alcove, we may presume, was sacred to the god who presided over gardens and country places; as in it was found a most beautiful and exquisitely wrought bronze tripod, supported by satyrs, with symbols emblematical of that deity: it is now transferred to the private room in the Royal Museum at Naples.

Pan, whose feast was in the same month as the feralia,[1] was probably here worshipped.

Within this recess was found a human skeleton, of which the hand still grasped a lance. Conjecture has imagined this the remains of a sentinel, who preferred dying at his post to quitting it for the more ignominious death, which, in conformity with the severe discipline of his country, would have awaited him.

It may be remarked, that the street of the tombs, as far as hitherto discovered, contains the monuments of those alone who had borne some office in the state, and that in most cases the ground on which they are respectively erected was assigned by vote of the public. From the latter circumstance it may be inferred, that this quarter was especially reserved for that purpose, while we may presume that the places appropriated for general sepulture were more removed from the city.

It may also be observed, that these sepulchres are only on the east side of Pompeii. Livy informs us, that

---

[1] February 15.

when Hannibal had planned the taking of the city of Tarentum, by the preconcerted treachery of Philumenos, an inhabitant, he was to approach that city towards the east, to the gate called Temenida; and at this gate were the tombs of the Tarentines.

About a furlong distant from the gate towards Herculaneum, is the villa which has been named Suburbana, excavated in 1775: the entrance is from the road or street of the tombs: at it were found the skeletons of two individuals; one held a purse containing many coins and medals, with the key of the door, and he still bore a ring, which indicated the equestrian rank. His companion had probably attempted to escape with some portable moveables and vases of bronze, found near them.[1] This house, placed upon the edge of the declivity which slopes towards the sea, consisted partly of two stories, the upper on the level of the street. It was spacious, and near the entrance was a bath with all the necessary appendages; in the rear the best rooms opened upon a terrace, running the whole width of the house, and overlooking a garden or xystus, about thirty yards square; this was surrounded by a covered walk or portico continued under the terrace; and beneath this again was a vaulted subterranean passage. At the further extremity a small temple, the roof of which was supported by six columns, projected towards the villa: and in its front a bath, or basin, occupied nearly the centre of the garden.

[1] Many other skeletons were found during the excavation of this street.

The lower apartments opening under the arcade were paved with mosaic, coved and beautifully painted; as also was the greater part of the villa. One of the rooms is said to have had a large glazed bow window; the glass was very thick, and deeply tinged with green: it was set in lead, like a modern casement.

In the subterranean passage were many large earthen wine vases, ranged in order against the walls: time had filled them with an earthy substance. Hither twenty-three of the family had betaken themselves for shelter and refuge. Various ornaments, as earrings, bracelets, were found with their skeletons; together with some few coins of gold, silver, and brass, chiefly of the emperor Galba, and the bones of the fingers of some still adhered to trifling articles they had wished to preserve. It is presumed that these individuals died from suffocation; since the volcanic matter here penetrated in so fine a powder, that the forms of their persons and apparel remained impressed in the indurated matter. The mould of the bosom of one is yet shown in the museum at Naples.[1]

In that part of the lower story removed from the covered portico, the rooms, more simply finished, contained spades, and other implements of husbandry: to this division of the house was a separate entrance.

---

[1] It was Sir William Hamilton's opinion, that this substance was deposited in a fluent state. The body in question was found some feet above the ancient level. She had probably struggled for some time against the continued showers of ashes, until sinking exhausted, she was covered with a slighter stratum, through which subsequent rains might have penetrated.

This has been called the villa of Cicero: M. Millin names it of Arrius Diomedes. The former, we know, had a house near Pompeii:[1] the latter was one of its magistrates; but there appears no real foundation for deciding this to have been the dwelling of either the one or the other.[2]

[1] Letters to Atticus.
[2] The plan is shown in Plate XI. See also Plates XX, XXI.

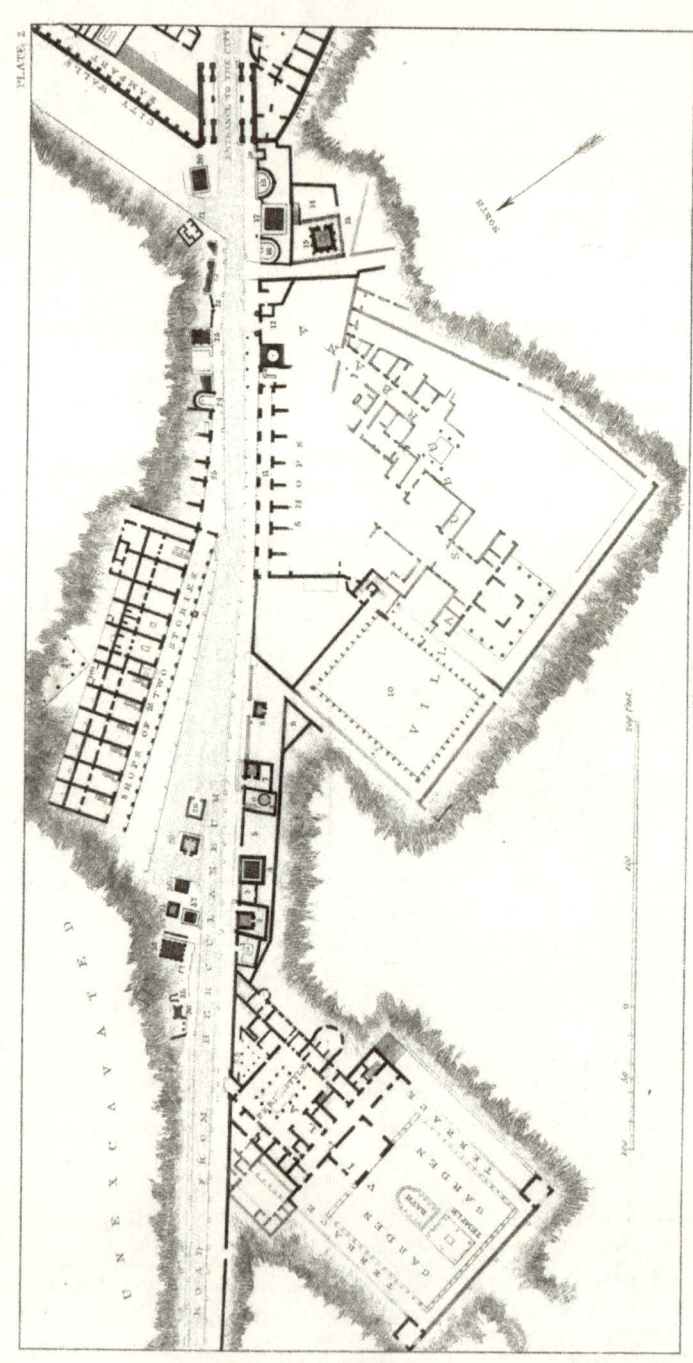

POMPEII.
STREET OF THE TOMBS.

PLATE II.

STREET OF THE TOMBS.

1. The Triclinium. This does not appear to have been the property of an individual; at least, no inscription remains to point out by whom it was prepared. The enclosed space was open to the sky; and the walls, covered with stucco, were painted in compartments.[1] A pediment raised on that next the street is one of the frequent instances of bad taste to be observed at Pompeii: under it was the entrance, little more than four feet high. Opposite, around three sides of a pedestal formed to sustain the table, was a raised seat, or bank, about 1 foot 9 inches in height, upon the inclined surface of which, lecti, or mattresses, were spread for the party to recline upon. This triclinium seems capable of affording space for nine persons, who were so placed, that the feet were kept on that part farthest removed from the front; the head of every succeeding individual being near the bosom of his neighbour. The table, which was removable at pleasure, was a great article of luxury and expense. It was frequently of silver, or curiously inlaid; being, both in this respect as well as in form, very similar to that used by the Turks and Greeks of the present day. Between the table and the doorway was a circular pedestal, or altar: here was made the offering to the infernal gods, who were propitiated on these occasions.

Triclinia, sometimes ornamented with columns, were

---

[1] Plate IV.

also erected for public dinners, or for the use of the priests and colleges.[1]

2. Adjoining the Triclinium is the tomb of Naevoleia Tyche, occupying nearly one side of a small enclosure, or septum, in which it is placed, leaving barely space sufficient to pass to its rear, where is the entrance to the interior by a wooden, open-framed door.[2] The cippus, or pedestal with which the tomb is surmounted, raised upon two steps, is faced with marble, and sculptured upon three sides. On that next the street is an inscription, stating that Naevoleia Tyche, during her life, had raised it for herself and C. Munatius Faustus, Augustal,[3] and Paganus; to whom the decurions, with the concurrence of the people, decreed the honour of the Bisellium,[4] on account of his worth; and also for her and his freed-men and women.

NAEVOLEIA · I · LIB · TYCHE · SIBI · ET
C · MVNATIO · FAVSTO · AVG · ET · PAGANO
CVI · DECVRIONES · CONSENSV · POPVLI
BISELLIVM · OB · MERITA · EIVS · DECREVERVNT
HOC · MONIMENTVM · NAEVOLEIA · TYCHE · LIBERTIS · SVIS
LIBERTABVSQ · ET · C · MVNATI · FAVSTI · VIVA · FECIT

Under this was a basso-relievo of many figures, representing, perhaps, the customary offering to the infernal gods; and over the inscription was a portrait, probably

---

[1] Muratori, 119, 1. "Triclam cum columnis et mensis et maceria s. p. d. d."

[2] Plate V.

[3] The Augustals were magistrates elected by the decurions to hold jurisdiction over sacred matters. The learned differ as to their duties. Reinesius supposes them magistrates,—Walpole (see 'Herculanensia'), priests. But Trimalchio was augustal, though no priest. They were entitled to the fasces.

[4] To the Bisellium was attached the privilege of the best place at the shows, as well as some other advantages.

of Naevoleia herself. The latter forms part of a border surrounding the whole.

On the north side, a vessel is represented, the prow ornamented with an armed head; a man sits guiding the rudder. This has been taken to denote the profession of Munatius; but it is, perhaps, allegorical. The full sail may have been chosen to indicate the uninterrupted prosperity and success of his worldly career.[1] On the south side was the Bisellium with which he was honoured.

To the left of the entrance to the interior of the tomb is a small stele, bearing an inscription relative to one of the family.

C · MVNATVS
ATIMETVS · VIX ·
ANNIS · LVII

3. An enclosed space, about fifteen feet square, containing three stele: the tops of these are carved, in some measure, to represent heads,[2] a lock of hair being twisted towards the front, which is quite flat; upon this was probably painted a likeness of the person to whose memory it was placed. They very much resemble Turkish tombstones of the present day, surmounted with a carved turban. Two of them are inscribed:

NISTACIDIVS   NISTACIDIAE
HELENVS · PAG   SCAPIDI

In the front of the wall separating this enclosure from the street, is a panel, containing an inscription, by which we are informed that it is fifteen feet square, and was the burial-place of Nistacidius.

---

[1] See pp. 55-6.
[2] See vignette, page 59.

NISTACIDIO · HELENO
¹ PAG · PAGI · AVG
NISTACIDIO · JANVARIO
MESONIAE · SATVLLAE · IN · AGRO
PEDES · XV · IN · FRONTE · PEDES · XV

4. Tomb of Calventius Quietus, placed in the middle of an enclosure, about seventeen feet square, which it nearly fills. No entrance has been found to the interior. On the back wall a pediment is raised; in the tympanum, two winged figures are represented, supporting an uninscribed tablet. The monument or cippus itself, about 5 feet 6 inches in front, is faced with marble. From an inscription next the street, we learn that it was erected to Calventius Quietus, Augustal; to whom, for the faithful discharge of his duty, by the decree of the decurions, and popular vote, the honour of the Bisellium was given.

C · CALVENTIO · QVIETO ·
AVGVSTALI ·
HVIC · OB · MVNIFICENT · DECVRIONVM ·
DECRETO · ET · POPVLI · CONSENSV · BISELLII
HONOR · DATVS · EST ·

Underneath this is a representation of the Bisellium, included in the same panel, on each side of which is a narrow compartment or pilaster. The cippus has a richly ornamented cornice and base-moulding. On the sides, between pilasters similar to those of the front, are civic or oak wreaths.

---

[1] The 14 regions of Rome were, by Augustus, divided into 424 vici; over each of these was appointed a magister, whose office was somewhat similar to our constable. The pagus is by Tacitus distinguished from the vicus, of which it was probably a further division; or, possibly, the paganus pagi was, in the suburbs and country towns, an officer whose functions were similar to those of the magister vici of the city.—SUETONIUS—VICTOR—DIO. Paga was also a tomb.—ISIDOR, *in Gloss.*

5. A vacant space, about 33 feet in front, in which one small stele alone remains. Probably the ground was unappropriated.
6. This tomb, although uninscribed, is handsome, about 17 feet high; the exterior is of stucco. The space or area in which it is placed is not rectangular. The access to it from the street is through a narrow and low doorway, 3 feet 3 inches high. A flight of steps leads up to the rear, where another equally small door conducts to the interior, which, also circular, is about 6 feet in diameter. The walls, of tufa, stuccoed, are tastefully painted, and crowned with a dome of a singular bell-like form, on the flat top of which is painted a face, or Medusa. Some cinerary urns, of coarse earth, were found within.
7. Tomb of Scaurus.

This monument is the most singular and curious of all the tombs hitherto discovered at Pompeii, and remarkable in being covered with extremely low relievos,[1] painted, of gladiatorial combats. The gladiators of Ampliatus, whose names and fate appear to have been written over their likenesses, lions, bears, panthers, bulls, wolves, and rabbits, with dogs, stags, and nondescripts, all seem to have been brought upon the scene for the entertainment of the Pompeians, and satisfaction of Scaurus' ghost.

A marble slab was found near the tomb; on application, it appeared to have originally belonged thereto. It has been fixed in its place, and states, that the monument was erected by Scaurus to his son,[2] Aricius

---

[1] The paintings of modern Greece are thus relieved: γραπτοι τυποι was, probably, the ancient term employed to designate this species of japan-work. The tupoi were impressed or cast relievos, whether of metal or plaster.

" Σιδηρονω τοις δ'ασπιδος τυποις επην."—EURIP., *Phoiniss.*

[2] The first letter is supplied, but there can be little doubt of it.

Scaurus, duumvir[1] for justice, upon the ground the decurions had voted for that purpose; they having at the same time decreed, that an equestrian statue of him should be erected in the Forum, and also two thousand sesterces for the celebration of his funeral obsequies.[2]

*RICIO · A · F · MEN ·
SCAVRO
IIVIR · I · D
*ECVRIONES · LOCVM · MONVM ·
∞ ∞ IN · FVNERE · ET · STATVAM · EQVESTR
*ORO · PONENDAM · CENSVERVNT
SCAVRVS · PATER · FILIO

The access to this tomb is through a low door,[3] opening into a septum, 19 feet square, in one angle of which the monument, 12 feet 9 inches by 10 feet, is placed. It is entered by the side; the undecorated interior, about 7 feet square, is vaulted, and surrounded with small niches, four on each side, except that of entrance, where the space of two is occupied by the doorway. In the centre is a square pillar, which reaches to and supports the ceiling, leaving a space round of not more than two feet; it is pierced each way with a niche, perhaps for a lamp. An opening for light was opposite the door.[4]

[1] The duumvirs, so called from their number, were magistrates who, in corporate cities, exercised similar functions to the consuls at Rome. They were chosen from amongst the decurions, or senators.—CICERO—TACITUS. The qualification for the latter dignity was the possession of a hundred thousand sesterces; about 800 pounds.—PLINY. They were *conscripti;* the senators, *patres conscripti.*

[2] Human blood must have been cheap, when 16*l.* 2*s.* 11*d.* could produce so much upon the arena; but, as the stone is here broken, there might have been another thousand.

[3] Five feet 3 inches high, hardly 4 feet wide; the door of the tomb is 4 feet high, 2 feet 2½ inches wide; the enclosing wall is 7 feet high.

[4] Sylla was father-in-law to a Scaurus, who was a great corrupter of

8. A space of more than eighty feet in front next occurs. Upon it is placed a single tomb and small stele, of which the details are not remarkable: the former is unfinished. In the rear of this—
9. Is a triangular enclosed space, to which there does not appear to have been any entrance.
10. Garden, with a covered portico, belonging to a villa not fully uncovered. It may be observed, that the ground slopes south-westward from this, and affords a fine view of the sea.
11. Arcade, under which were shops.
12. Entrance to a villa. On each side the doorway are low, hollow, conical frustâ, apparently placed for the purpose of protection to the trunks of trees. Perhaps vines may have been trained over the columns in front of this doorway.
13. About this spot were two subterranean depositaries, now covered up, in which cinerary urns were discovered; one of glass, with a cover of the same material, was placed within another of baked earth, and the whole enveloped in a third of lead.
14. A space, through which was the way, by a flight of steps, to the tomb:
15. This was about 19 feet square, placed within an elevated area, surrounded by a dwarf wall, the upper part of which is pierced with small, circular-headed perforations, forming a sort of balustrade. Four fluted semicolumns on each of its sides upheld the epistylia and terra cotta roof. In the decoration of the latter, some representations of scenic masks, *personæ* of that material here found, were probably used.

Several ill-executed marble statues, now in the Royal Museum, were found in the interior, which was set round with niches. The walls were painted; in the

Roman manners. He built a theatre for 30,000 persons, with 3000 brass statues; and 360 columns, of which 120 were glass, 38 feet high.— PLINY, 36—24.

centre was a large pedestal. The exterior, with the columns of brick and rubble-work, coated with stucco, now much dilapidated, was originally handsome.

16. A semicircular seat, raised upon a high step. It is about 17 feet in diameter, and bears an inscription, which declares it to have been dedicated to the public priestess Mamia, daughter, perhaps, of Porcius, to whom the decurions had decreed a place of sepulture.

MAMIAE · P · F · SACERDOTI · PVBLICAE · LOCVS
SEPVLTVR · DATVS · DECVRIONVM · DECRETO

This inscription runs in one line of large letters round at the back of the seat, each extremity of which was carved with a representation of a lion's foot and claw.

17. Sepulchre, which, stripped of its external facing, exhibits only the rough masonry, placed upon a brown stone basement. Here was found a Doric frieze of the same material, which probably belonged to this monument. Between it and the seat last mentioned, upon a small block, is an inscription, stating that a space, 25 feet square, had been decreed by the decurions for the place of sepulture of M. Porcius.

M · PORC · M · F
EX · DEC · DECRETO
IN · FRONTEM · P · XXV
IN · AGRO · PED · XXV

The space occupied by this tomb, or rather that between the two semicircular seats, is about this dimension.

Some of the scattered fragments found about this quarter formed, doubtless, the more ornamented exterior of the tomb of M. Porcius; though we are inclined to conjecture, that it was never completed. An inscription in the theatre informs us that Marcus Porcius, son of Marcus Porcius, was one of the duumvirs to whom was committed the superintendence, and funds for the erection, of the covered theatre. Prompted by this service, the decurions, perhaps, decreed him a place of sepulture, which was marked out by the memorandum in question, placed at one corner of the ground selected. We may imagine Marcus Porcius erecting to himself posthumous celebrity, and, in composing epitaphs, consuming that time which was fast advancing to swallow up him and his community for ever.

18. Semicircular seat, raised upon two steps; it is about 21 feet in diameter, and bore an inscription, now in the Royal Museum. Each extremity of this seat is finished with a gryphon's leg and claw.
19. Alcove of the rural deity. The interior was painted in fresco, in compartments. Upon a pedestal in the centre was found the tripod mentioned at page 63, as also a human skeleton.
20. Pedestal of stone, which is said to have sustained a colossal statue; the mouldings of the base are of white marble.
21. Branch of the road to Nola.

Several tombs, or ornamented structures, were erected about this spot, the exact forms of some of which cannot now be ascertained, while others leave not room even for conjecture. Amongst them were a circular edifice of stone, adorned with columns, and a cylindrical stele, or cippus, 8 feet high, of the same material.

23. Tomb, faced with stucco, upon a basement of stone. A long slab, probably bearing an inscription, appears to have occupied the space between the two angular pilasters, in the principal front. Between the three pilasters of the side were suspended festoons. From this tomb, towards the entrance to the city, ran a wall of opus reticulatum, in which were inserted two altars, marked, on the plan, 22.
24. An arched alcove. The semicircular end is covered

with a semi-dome; the whole interior is painted; and a seat runs round the inside. This recess appears to have had a similar destination with that on the right of the entrance to the city.

25. Shops.
26. Arcade, under which were shops; above is a terrace, with others, and the part of a house, 27.
28. Enclosed space, dividing the two roads. The insulated situation of this would probably justify the conjecture, that it was an ustrina, or unwrought[1] foundation for the erection of the funeral piles. Cicero informs us, that the law forbade their being erected within sixty feet of any house, without the consent of the owner; but if the latter allowed it to be completed without opposition, no ground for action could lie.[2]
29. Tomb, of which the exterior is much dilapidated. Opposite the door was a niche, and over this an opening for light. In the arched interior, several vases were found. The door is curious, being of marble, little more than 3 feet high, 2 feet 9 inches wide, $4\frac{1}{2}$ inches thick, and moved on pivots formed out of the same block. Doors thus constructed seldom opened without noise.[3]
30, 31. Ruined sepulchres.
32. A well-executed tomb, in stone, of simple form, about 15 feet high. Upon two of its sides are similar inscriptions, which inform us that it was erected by Alleia Decimilla, public priestess of Ceres, to her husband, Luccius Libella, ædile,[4] duumvir, and quinquennial prefect; also to her son, M. Alleius Libella,

---

[1] The pile was unwrought.—CICERO, *Leg*. Sylla was the first patrician burnt.

[2] Tombs were sometimes erected, imitating the funeral pile. Many still exist in Asia Minor, of marble.

[3] Hence, "Graviter crepuere fores."—TERENCE, *passim*.

[4] Amongst other matters, the ædiles had the care of the public buildings, and provided the shows.

dccurion at 17, upon ground decreed by the public for that purpose.

M · ALLEIO · LVCCIO · LIBELLAE · PATRI · AEDILI
IIVIR · PRAEFECTO · QVINQ · ET · M · ALLEIO · LIBELLAE · F ·
DECVRIONI · VIXIT · ANNIS · XVII · LOCVS · MONVMENTI
PVBLICE · DATVS · EST · ALLEIA · M · F · DECIMILLA · SACERDOS
PVBLICA · CERERIS · FACIVNDVM · CVRAVIT · VIRO · ET · FILIO

33. Tomb of Lucius Ceius, son of Lucius, and Lucius Labeon, twice quinquennial duumvir for justice. It was placed to them by Menomachus, who, it seems, had it very ill executed, of rubble-work and stucco.[1]

L · CEIO · L · F · MEN · L · LABEONI
ITER · D · V · I · D · QVINQ
MENOMACHVS · L ·

The legs of a warrior, and shield, almost the size of life, are seen upon one of its sides; but it is now very much defaced. It also bore other painted inscriptions, now totally obliterated; and a piece of a statue, which seemed a portrait, in white marble, was found near.

A small tomb, to the left of this, was probably in some way connected with it.

34. Dilapidated tomb.
35. Sepulchral niche, having a seat within, and stele formed for a face. The inside is painted; the top a semi-dome. By an inscription we learn that it was erected to Velasius Gratus, who lived twelve years. Upon the stele is inscribed,

IVNONI
TYCHES · IVLIAE
AVGVSTAE · VENER ·

---

[1] If there was a restriction as to expense, the intention was, probably, to have as large a display as possible for the prescribed sum.

78 POMPEIANA.

36. Tombs of the family of Arrius: one continued podium forms a sub-basement to these tombs, as well as to that of L. Ceius. In front of the podium is an inscription:

ARRIAE · M · F ·
DIOMEDES · L · SIBI · SVIS

The sepulchre of M. Arrius Diomedes, constructed of rubble-work, is faced with stucco: two fasces are represented upon its front. Over them, in a panel, is an inscription, recording the dedication of the tomb to the use of himself and family:

M · ARRIVS · DIOMEDES ·
SIBI · SVIS · MEMORIAE
MAGISTER · PAG · AVG · FELICI · SVBVRB

Two children, a male and a female, of Diomedes, are commemorated by two blocks, each bearing an inscription. Arria was eight years old: respecting the son we are only informed, that he was the first-born.

ARRIAE · M · F   M · ARRIO
VIII   PRIMOGENI

Engraved by Chas. Heath.

PEMBROKE.

PLATE III

Offers a view of a scene which has no parallel. Remote antiquity is here combined with an air of newness which appears but the work of yesterday. "Non est quod nos tumulis metiaris, et his monumentis quæ viam disparia prætexunt."[1]

The monuments represented in this view were excavated under Murat: some of them originally, in all probability, sustained statues; but these latter may have been removed immediately after the destruction of the city, as they must partly have appeared above the soil.[2]

The first door-way to the right, under a pediment, is the entrance to the triclinium: after which appears the cippus, surmounting the tomb of Naevoleia Tyche (2);[3] the door-way of entrance to the septum, or little court, in which it is placed, may be observed.[4] A small enclosed space, to which there is no entrance, next occurs, before the tomb of Calventius Quietus, which bears the second cippus (4). The round pedestal which follows is uninscribed; and the tomb of Scaurus is the last of the series. The remains of two rough stone statues, found during the excavations, are placed against the wall of the triclinium and enclosure of Naevoleia. The raised bank, or seat, between the foot-way and tombs, was covered with cement.

---

[1] SENECA.

[2] Tombs were frequently terminated in this manner. One of the supposed monuments to Scipio at Liternum had his statue so placed.—LIVY.

[3] The figures refer to the plan of the street, Plate II.

[4] See Plate V. The interior is shown, Plate VI.

On the left are seen the tops of the two stele[1] of the children of Arrius Diomedes; whose tomb appears over them (36).

> " . . . . οστεα δ'αυτων
> Χρυσεω εν κρητηρι θεσαν, περι δε σφισι σημα
> Εσσομενα τευξαντο· θεσαν δ'αρα δοιω υπερθεν
> Στηλας."—SMYRNÆUS, 10, 485.

The next in order is the tomb (33) of Luccius Ceius; while the simple pedestal of Alleia Decimilla, public priestess of Ceres, intercepts the view of half the entrance to the city.

It may be remarked that the volcanic stone pavement of the road is apt to take a conchoidal fracture.

The pedestal of Decimilla is sixteen feet high. The figures are without character, introduced merely for the purpose of giving some idea of the scale; but they have no business at Pompeii, where the associations are of two thousand years since.

> "Here pensive contemplation loves to linger,
> And people all the silent solitude
> With the conceptions of the soul within."
> SOTHEBY.

---

[1] These sort of tombstones were to be bought in the shops of the lapidarii, ready prepared to receive the likeness of any one to whom a monument was required. A piece of this sort remains in the Vatican: the heads are in block.

POMPEII.

THE SEPULCHRAL TRICLINIUM

ENTRANCE to the TOMB of NAEVOLEIA TYCHE.

PLATE 6

Engraved by C. Heath.

POMPEII.

PLATE IV.

View of the inside of the sepulchral triclinium, with the side of the cippus of Naevoleia Tyche; on which is the representation of a ship, alluded to in pages 68-9.

The painting upon the walls, and even the stucco, has now almost wholly disappeared.

PLATE V.

Entrance to the tomb of Naevoleia Tyche.

The spectator is supposed to be within the small court in which the tomb is placed.

The wooden door is restored from observation of the ancient remains. The back of the cippus is left unornamented; at the side is the Bisellium. In the left-hand corner is the stele of Munatus.

Through the entrance is seen the lower part of the pedestal of Alleia Decimilla.

PLATE VI.

Interior of the tomb of Naevoleia Tyche.

This was about 6 feet 6 inches square, ill stuccoed, arched, and niches formed around for the reception of cinerary urns. Some were of coarse earth; three others, about 15 inches high, were of glass, and contained bones, with a liquid, which, upon analysis, was considered to be composed of water, wine, and oil. Each had a lamp, and piece of money for Charon: more lamps were ready in a corner; they were of red common earth.

A small aperture, as represented, was left for light.

PLATE VII.

View across the Street of the Tombs.

The ruined tomb in the fore-ground is stripped of the ornamental exterior: it is marked on the plan 29, and is shown, Plate X. For the other tombs see Plate VIII.

PLATE VIII.

This view comprises the tombs of Scaurus. The circular uninscribed tomb, with those of Calventius Quietus and of Naevoleia Tyche. A vacant space occurs between the second and third, probably reserved for the purpose of future honour to some personage, and might in the interim have been planted with trees. The gladiatorial combats[1] upon the tomb of Scaurus have been spoken

---

[1] These, except that over the door, had all fallen, Jan. 1818.

VIEW across the STREET of the TOMBS.

Engraved by Chas. Booth.

POMPEII.

of, page 71. Horace probably alludes to such representation in the following lines :

> ". . . . . . . Fulvî Rutubæque
> Aut Placideiani, contento poplite miror
> Prælia, rubrica picta aut carbone; velut si
> Re vera pugnent, feriant, vitentque moventes
> Arma viri."

It has been questioned whether the inscription applied to this tomb originally belonged to it. The slab upon which it is engraved certainly fits the place, although not there found: at all events the matter cannot be worth controversy. This monument, as well as its cylindrical neighbour, was probably surmounted with a statue. The hole in the latter was originally a panel, intended, perhaps, to bear an inscription. It has been broken in.

The pediment upon the rear of the maceria of Calventius Quietus, and figures supporting an uninscribed tablet, will be observed. Between this tomb and that of Naevoleia, is the panel in the wall containing the inscription, page 69.

The little acroteria, in some instances bearing bassi relievi, and which appear so frequent about these sepulchres, are curious. Some tombs remaining in the necropolis of the ancient city of Cnidus are ornamented in a similar manner. Places of sepulture were originally surrounded with a fence or paling of wood; the standards at intervals, so necessary for its stability, were possibly the prototypes of these pinnacles: and from them were probably suspended the garlands and wreaths with which, at stated periods, the sepulchre was adorned. The smallness of the door-ways has been before noticed. The second is only 3 feet 3 inches high.

PLATE IX.

This view shows the rear of the cylindrical tomb and that of Scaurus, with the entrances to their interior. Across the street is seen the continued arcade, under which were shops. The arches above these are of another terrace of houses.

PLATE X.

Outlines of the insulated tomb (29).
A The plan. B The elevation. C Section, showing the niche opposite the door, over which was an opening for light. D Section longitudinally. E The marble door, which moved upon pivots, with a handle and fastening. F Plan of the door. G A vase: another vase, of oriental alabaster, with handles, remains in the tomb, containing bones and ashes. A gold ring was also found, set with a sapphirine agate, tolerably cut, with a stag scratching itself. A low seat ran round, upon which were urns of glass, little bottles of the same material, and an altar of pottery.[1]

---

[1] These details are taken from Mazois.

Engraved by J. Smory.

POMPEII.

BACK OF THE TOMB OF SCAURUS.

PLATE 10.

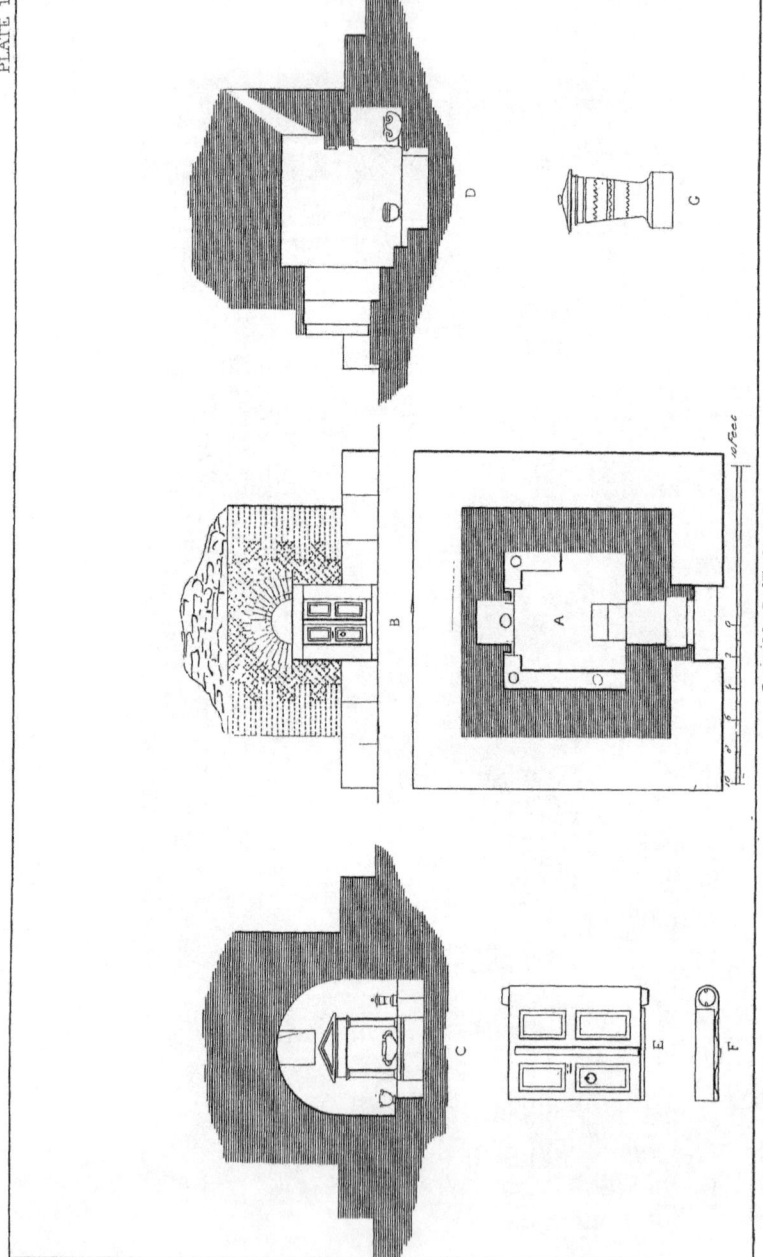

Engraved by Chas Heath.

POMPEII.

Engraved by Chas Heath.

POMPEII.

PLATE 12.

Engraved by Chas Heath.

POMPEII.

PLATE XI.

Side view of the tomb of C. Quietus, looking towards Vesuvius.

The spectator is supposed to be placed in the area of the uninscribed cylindrical tomb. The tomb of Naevoleia Tyche is hidden by that of C. Quietus, which occupies the left of the view. The distant monument is of Arrius; beyond which are the stele of his children. The small alcove of Velasius occurs between this tomb and that of Luccius Ceius, great part of which is concealed by the pedestal of the public priestess Alleia Decimilla. Some ruined tombs, and part of the enclosure, supposed to have been the ustrina for funeral piles, appear on the right.

PLATE XII.

View from the seat of Mamia back from the gate towards Herculaneum. The two altars or pedestals upon the right are marked upon the plan (22). Over them is an uninscribed tomb. The slab which bore the inscription seems to have been inserted under the capitals of the two centre pilasters; but it has not been found.

The ornament of the festoon probably alluded to the custom of adorning the tomb with flowers.[1]

---

[1] "Πανκαρπιος στεφανος."—CUPER, *Mon. Ant.*, 220.

The alcove (24) next occurs, covered with a semi-dome. On the outside the archivolt springs from the capital of the pilaster, without the intervention of an entablature.[1] The tiled top is modern, and placed for the preservation of the structure. After a few shops was the entrance to the arcade, under which were other shops.

In the fore-ground are some ornamental fragments; but of what edifices they formed a part, it is no longer possible to ascertain. Many sepulchres are much dilapidated in this quarter: to some of them the remains in question doubtless belonged.

---

[1] The ruins of Spalatro were by Whittington supposed to exhibit the earliest specimen of this.

WALLS.

The walls of Pompeii are, perhaps, the only part of the city at all calculated to resist that rapid decay, which seems to hasten the disappearance of every other remain within their circuit. They are built with a receding face, of large stones, sometimes four to five feet long, laid in horizontal beds; the joints between the blocks in each course not preserved upright, but inclining more or less to the plane of the horizon:[1] a style of masonry

---

[1] This masonry is not unusual in Greece; it occasioned some little saving of material.

The walls are of Piperino, with the exception of the lower four or five courses, which are of Travertino. Marks for recognition, in the Oscan cha-

common to many of the Etruscan cities, amongst which Volterra affords other points of similarity.

They are partly well put together; but with an extraordinary admixture of rubble-work, and predominance of the species of brick-work called reticulatum, exhibiting an appearance strongly resembling that of certain modern Turkish fortresses; where the works, originally Greek, and well constructed, have descended through a series of barbarous possessors, and undergone many centuries of ill-judged repairs.[1]

Towers are placed at unequal intervals, twenty-seven feet by thirty-three, projecting forward seven, and composed of rubble walls, three feet in thickness, in three stories. Between them, supported by a double wall, ranged the ramparts; the whole nearly twenty feet wide, including the two walls, and varying in height from the ground twenty-five to thirty, according to the local level. They communicated through the towers by arched doorways on the third or upper story.[2]

racter, are frequent upon the blocks. It is singular that similar characters, or rather similar rude mæanders, are seen upon the vases lately found under the stratum of Piperino near Albano, which some have imagined anterior to the extinction of the volcanoes near Rome. Their history is briefly, that the surveyors employed in the beginning of the year 1817 in making a road, on cutting away the Piperino, found many nails buried in the mass, some four inches long. Under the stratum were discovered rough terra cotta vases: they were very little below the under side of the Piperino. It has been thence inferred, that the stratum must have been in some way undermined for placing them.

[1] Frequently over the bad work occur three or four courses of regular masonry, in good blocks.

[2] Mons. Mazois, in his magnificent work, to which the reader may refer for more detailed information respecting the walls, as well as every other

Embattled parapets were raised upon the outer and inner edge of the rampart: they formed, in appearance, a double line of defence to the town; that nearest the city being some feet higher than the outer. They were built of large stones, about two feet six inches thick: to each battlement a shoulder returned inwards, affording an additional security to the defender.[1] This double wall admitting a wide rampart, is considered by Vitruvius much superior to the ordinary mode, where a single one only was used.[2] Of the latter description seems to have been that on the south side of Pompeii.

The outer wall of the towers appears invariably to have fallen. It may be conjectured, while history is silent as to the fate of this city, upon the termination of the Marsic war, in which it was a principal, that Sylla at least dismantled the fortress; and that this was the plan pursued by the dictator to render the fortifications useless. After the ramparts were occupied, the superior height of the inner parapet would have prevented an enemy from immediately entering the town until the tower was taken; whereas, by throwing down the outer wall of the latter, possession of the ramparts was unnecessary, and the city became indefensible.

In the reign of Titus, the Romans had long since

part of Pompeii, remarks, that the walls never make a decided angle; a principle laid down by Vitruvius, who, Lib. I, 5, considers angles to favour considerably the assailants. Urbes ab Orbes.—Festus.

[1] Sometimes in Greece a connecting course runs over the whole battlements, making their appearance like openings for windows.

[2] This rampart obviated the necessity for the frequent recurrence of towers.

ceased to fear the irruptions of a foreign enemy, while the policy of the emperors would naturally prompt them to diminish the chances of success to domestic treason. In ancient, as well as modern times, the god Terminus always carried the national defences to the extended boundary. The Goths, the Suevi, the Persians, found few obstacles to the progress of victory, after passing the frontiers; Athens was conquered at the extremity of the Euxine; Spain was traversed by the conquerors on the Rhine; and the people of Antioch in their theatre were awakened from the dream of security by an enemy whom they imagined still beyond the Euphrates.

The nature of the repairs which have taken place in various parts seem also to point out, that the fortress had thus, for some length of time, been kept up more for appearance than apprehension of attack; bad brick and rubble being used for this purpose throughout the fortification, and by means of stucco made to resemble the better constructed masonry of the original wall.[1]

The site of the south wall seems generally occupied by houses placed upon the edge of the declivity which slopes thence towards the sea.

Five principal entrances have been discovered to the city, two of which only are worthy of notice. The principal, towards Herculaneum and Naples, before spoken of, is about forty-seven feet in depth; its whole extent forty-two. It consisted of an outer and an inner wall,[2] each perforated with three arched openings; the

---

[1] This stucco is of extraordinary perfection of surface and quality.

[2] Built of brick and rubble, in alternate courses.

intermediate space being probably left open to the sky, except the lateral ways for foot passengers, which communicated with the uncovered area in the centre, by two arched openings on each side. A portcullis closed the centre archway, about seven feet distant from the front; and, with another gate on the inside, formed a double security.

A gate of Tarentum, mentioned in Livy, seems to have been planned in this manner: as we there find the conspirators by stratagem passing the outer, and, after putting to death the sentinel, forcing the inner gate of the city.[1]

The whole building was rather advanced; being placed at an acute angle, formed by the walls of the city.

The gate now called of Nola, but which faced the passage of the Sarnus, is on the north-east side of the city. It is not placed at right angles with that part of the wall in which it is inserted, but in a line with the street communicating therewith, and, unlike that of Herculaneum, is retired from the face of the fortification. Two towers were constructed, guarding the entrance of a sort of passage between two parallel walls, leading to the gateway: which has but one arch, twenty-one feet high and twelve wide; the gate being placed four feet within it, or about fifty from the face of the external walls.

The very ancient gate of the Lions at Mycene is built on this plan; by which the attacking party, who could only advance in small numbers, would, (cooped up in a

---

[1] See also Polybius, who calls the outer gate ρινοπυλη.

passage little wider than the gateway they approached,) be exposed to great disadvantage and annoyance from the besieged lining the tops of the flanking walls.

The city was possibly more liable to attack upon this than any other quarter.

This gateway also is built of rubble and bricks, covered with stucco. The key stone of the arch towards the city is carved with the representation of a human head; and at the side of this latter is placed a curious Oscan inscription.[1] These, as well as the flanking towers, are possibly coeval with the earliest part of the walls, and here placed when the present less ancient gateway was formed.

The entrance to the Etruscan city Volterra, towards the country, has a similar key stone; in addition to which the arch springs from two other colossal heads.[2] In the Museum of that city is an alabaster vase, representing the death of Capaneus with a similar gateway; though the artist probably copied that of his native town instead of the more appropriate entrance to Thebes. The inscription reads,[3]

F · PVPIDIIS · F · MED · TVF · AAMANAPHPHED
ISIDV · PRVPHATTED

---

[1] Oscan is supposed to have been the language of the lower orders.

[2] Mr. Walpole, 'Anecdotes of Painting,' attributes the invention of ornamented corbels to Marchion of Arezzo.

[3] See the tail-piece to this section. The first letter is evidently a digamma. With reference to the office named, Livy informs us that the chief magistrate of the Campanians was called Meddixtuticus, *minister of public safety?*

By this we are informed that it was repaired and dedicated to Isis by the Meddixtuticus Popidius.

meddix looks like *curator*, whence perhaps the Latin *medicus:* pronounced like the orthography of the inscription o mērico by the modern Neapolitans; who seem not to have corrupted, but retained the ancient sound. They also say *taldi* for *tardi,* and on the contrary, *corpa* for *colpa.* According to Cicero, Quinctilian, and Macrobius, the R had taken place frequently of the more ancient S: as in Papirius, originally Papisius. There was possibly another name at the beginning of this inscription, as the *aamanaphpher* and *pruphatter* look like plural formations, for although in Livy there appears to have been but one Meddixtuticus, yet we have another authority for the existence of two.—*Enn. ap. Fest.*

PLATE XIII.

View of the entrance to the city from Herculaneum. On the right is the uninscribed semi-circular seat (18): between which and the gate is the alcove wherein was found a skeleton with a spear. Opposite is the pedestal, supposed to have sustained a bronze colossal or equestrian statue.

The centre arch of the gateway no longer exists, but the two side entrances remain perfect. The Ionic columns, represented against that on the left, do not appear there in any of the early views; although the oldest Ciceroni on the spot declare they were there found. They are now placed against the pedestal on the left, and in all probability formed part of the decoration of some tomb, and not of this gateway.

Near this entrance was found a sun-dial, of marble, very similar to one brought from Athens by the Earl of Elgin, which is deposited in the British Museum.

PLATE XIV.

The foregoing gateway, as seen from the side next the city. On the right is the entrance to an inn, or post-house; chequers are exhibited at the side of the door-way. The bones of horses were found in the stables; and in the cellar, large earthen vases for wine. Rings for tying the horses, and three cars were found; the wheels

Engraved by Chas H Eath.

POMPEII.

OUTSIDE OF THE GATE OF HERCULANEUM.

POMPEII.

INSIDE OF THE GATE OF HERCULANEUM.

POMPEII.
GATE OF NOLA OUTSIDE.

light, and dished much like the modern, 4 feet 3 inches diameter, ten spokes, a little thicker at each end. In the yard were two fountains.

On the first excavation of the opposite house, it was considered, from the sign exhibited, to have been a fornix, or lodging-house; but the subsequent discovery of similar emblemata in less doubtful situations, one in a bake-house, have served to show that the display of the symbols of divinities do not always identify the spot with their worship.

The house between this and the gateway is said to have been that of an apothecary.

Guard stones for mounting horses were placed, by the law of C. Gracchus de viis muniendis. The holes may here be observed in the curb for passing the halter.

PLATE XV.

View of the entrance to Pompeii from the north-east. Towards the city is the wrought key-stone, and Oscan inscription.[1] The rise of the ground is very quick up to the gateway. In the fore-ground, to the right, is seen a piece of the cornice which crowned the tower above.[2] Against this the wall of the city abuts in an obtuse, and runs off at an acute angle.

---

[1] *Vide* pages 92 and 98.

[2] M. Mazois does not suppose these to have been towers, but the foundations of another gateway.

PLATE XVI.

WALLS OF THE CITY.

At the second tower from the spectator is seen the sally-port. The front wall, which was stuccoed, with a flat face, is, as usual, demolished. The returns are rusticated in the same material. The ramparts communicate through the towers by arches. In the left corner is the lower part of a battlement. The stucco is of extraordinary perfection and smoothness of surface.

PLATE XVII.

In the upper part may be observed the arched doorway, conducting through the lower stories to the sally-port, by a staircase constructed in that part of the tower which projected towards the city, so as to leave the communication free from rampart to rampart. Three of the stone spouts, to convey the water from the latter, are visible. None of the battlements remain entire in any part shown in these two views.

POMPEII.
WALLS OF THE CITY.

POMPEII.
VIEW OF ONE OF THE TOWERS FROM THE OUTSIDE.

POMPEII.

VARIOUS ORNAMENTS FROM NEAR THE GATE OF NOLA.

PLATE XVIII.

Is compiled from remains found in the street of the Nolan Gate. The centre compartment (4) is an altar, above which is a painting of a sacrifice.

These paintings of serpents, but generally in pairs, are frequently seen at the angles and corner of streets at Pompeii. They were the local genii;[1] and their emblems rendered the spot sacred, and guarded it from pollution:

> ". . . . hic . . veto quisquam faxit oletum
> Pinge duos angues. Pueri, sacer est locus; extra
> Meiite." PERSEUS, 1, 112.

It is remarkable that the serpent was in all histories mysterious. The serpent of Eve need not be cited; a serpent originally delivered the Delphic responses; it was the emblem of eternity; as was, perhaps, the cone, or germ, like the egg of inert matter.[2]

1 Outline of a painting, representing a combat between two gladiators. Their helmets and boots are brazen; the former has eye holes; the plumes blue. Lipsius says, only the Samnites were crested. They wear a red tunic, or subligaculum, with a bronze or leathern belt; their legs armed with ochrea. The left arm was left to the shield alone for defence.

2. Are gryphons painted upon a wall.
3. Is also a painted ornament upon a pilaster.

---

[1] See 'Antichità d'Ercolano,' vol. ii, where the addition of Harpocrates imposed even silence.—LAMPRIDIUS, *in Heliogab.*—SERVIUS.

In modern Italy the same purpose is answered by a Madonna, or saint.

[2] MACROBIUS, Sat. I, 19—20.

98 POMPEIANA.

4. Border of a room painted in fresco. The ornaments are shaded upon a green ground, except a part shown darker, which is red; the darkest tint is blue.
5. Is a similar border; ground yellow, ornaments brown and red.

PLATE XIX

Is an attempt to give some idea of the principal entrance to Pompeii, as it once existed.

The gateway is restored in the simplest manner possible, but the biga over it is imaginary. Of the walls there can be no question. The pedestal supporting a statue on the left undoubtedly was built for that purpose; but it possibly might have been an equestrian or other group, since the plan of the pedestal is not square. The statue is from one found in the city. Under it is a road, supposed to have branched off to Nola; another on the right, conducted to the sea. Over the latter is the monument (15); before this the seat of the priestess Mamia, which is separated from another semi-circular seat by a tomb (17). The Ædiculum joins the gateway.

As a general observation, it may be remarked that in this view everything beneath the horizontal line is certain; above it, only partly so.

POMPEII.

ENTRANCE TO THE CITY FROM HERCULANEUM RESTORED.

DOMESTIC ARCHITECTURE.

The houses of Pompeii remain preserved to us in a state that leaves little to be desired upon the subject of many of those minor details, with which, until the discovery of that city, we were almost wholly unacquainted; and although no dwelling hitherto excavated could vie in extent with the magnificent villas which belonged to Pliny or Lucullus, and still less with the splendid imperial residence, yet, by comparing their remains with the ordinary houses, as described by Vitruvius, we shall find them fully adequate to enable us to form a tolerably accurate idea of the domestic architecture of the inhabitants, if not of the beauty and order of the more costly edifices of Rome.

A great feature in the arrangement of the ancient house, as distinguished from the modern, was the internal court. Courts were usually formed, each surrounded with apartments, which, lighted from within, at first sight seem to have afforded little possibility of the domestic concerns of the family being overlooked by any one not included within the walls. But this was an advantage they did not really possess, as we may conclude from Plautus;[1] and Seneca speaks of the annoyance the neighbours were subject to, from the disorderly luxury of those who, changing night into day, indulged in the false refinement and late hours of the age.

Many causes for the houses having acquired this form may be conjectured. In the early ages of society, each might be considered as representing a small city or community, to which the surrounding wall gave security:[2] and subsequently, when every man assumed the right of overlooking his more wealthy neighbour, when any departure from a frugality ordained by law was considered criminal, it became necessary to the pro-

---

[1] " Forte fortuna per impluvium huc despexi in proxumum,
　Atque ego illam aspicio osculantem Philocomasium cum altero
　Nescio quo adolescente."

Mil. Glor. 2—3.

[2] Houses were sometimes made very strong. Publius Verus was accused of a design upon the liberties of the people for the manner in which he built his house upon the Velian hill.—LIVY, V, 42.

prietor to secure himself against the misrepresentations of his private enemies.

A jealousy, also, somewhat approaching that of the modern Eastern nations, seems to have prevailed towards the female part of the family, to whom the most remote portion of the house was appropriated; an inner court, around which their rooms were distributed, was only accessible through another, where a similar arrangement existed for the accommodation of the men and servants. That this was the plan of the ancient Greeks may be gathered from Homer, who thus places the thalamoi of the daughters of Priam within the royal palace; and it was over the wall enclosing the aule that Phœnix, eluding the vigilance of the guards placed over him, made his escape, without alarming either them or the women whose apartments he had passed.

In the Odyssey, Helen bids her maids prepare a bed for Telemachus under the portico of the outer court. They, bearing lights, proceed from the inner to obey her commands: accordingly, Telemachus and the son of Nestor pass the night in the former, while Menelaus and Helen occupy the latter division of the house.

In Terence, Jupiter passes over the neighbours' roofs, and descends through the impluvium to Danaë; thereby avoiding the men's apartments, through whose court he must have passed had he got into the house from the street.[1]

The houses of the early Romans were small; and the

---

[1] "Atque per alienas tegulas venisse clanculum per impluvium mulieri."

doors were left unclosed during the single meal which sufficed for the day, that it might be seen no one exceeded the bounds of frugality prescribed by the laws. But as civilisation advanced, and luxury was introduced, their size enlarged to the excess, that four hundred slaves[1] do not appear to have been an extraordinary number to be included under one roof. The tops were shaded with trees and laid out in gardens; while in the interior the decorations of the room changed with the courses of the feast.[2] Augustus, whose policy would never allow him to indulge in this extravagance, at length restricted their height to seventy feet; an elevation which appears sufficient, but for exceeding which many were afterwards accused and fined. And thus the irregularity of the capital became so great, that the calamity might have been considered a public good which made way for the judicious plans of the emperor Nero, who, passionately fond of building, first made Rome a regular city. He ordained that each house should be surrounded by its own wall: but some thought that regulating the width and disposition of the street, and heights of the houses, by lessening the shade, did not conduce to the health of the inhabitants.[3] Pompeii remained, to its fall, a city of lanes rather than streets.

The general uniformity of plan still admitted con-

[1] TACITUS.—They were all executed for not preventing the murder of their master. Within the walls of one house was frequently produced every article of life.

[2] SENECA. [3] TACITUS.

siderable variety in the detail; but they were all attended with imperfections repugnant to modern ideas of taste and conveniency. The absence of chimneys entirely, and windows generally, may be particularly noticed. The only light received in the rooms was through an aperture formed in or over the door; and even this was borrowed. But we are to recollect that the Romans were not a "Genus ignavum qui tecto gaudet et umbrâ:"[1] not a domestic people. Their society was to be sought in the Forum, and public porticoes.

Vitruvius is almost the only writer of antiquity who gives any real information respecting the houses of the ancients; for the casual mention by others of various parts of their dwellings cannot be considered precise; and even the very detailed description we have from Pliny of his villas, although that of an advocate, yet being written in a letter to a friend, and intended rather to give an idea of their comforts and beauties, than architectural arrangement, of course would not be so exact as that of one whose profession was architecture, and intention to give an accurate account of such edifices as were best adapted to the customs of his time, with their proper and most approved proportions.

Pompeii offers advantages to the more modern antiquary, of which his predecessors were not in possession. It contains houses, built and inhabited by Romans of the time in which Vitruvius wrote. By his assistance we may therefore at least hope to ascertain pretty nearly

---

[1] JUVENAL.

the name by which each apartment was designated, if we are not enabled to clear his text from the many obscurities with which his commentators have loaded him.

The part of the house first described is the atrium[1] and cavædium. After saying there are five kinds of cavædia, he proceeds to state the proportions of the atrium with its alæ on the right and left, the tablinum and the fauces: the dimensions of the latter arise from those given to the tablinum. These are on the breadth of the atrium, while the alæ are on each side, or length.

From the fauces he passes to the peristyle and triclinium, the oici, the exedra, and pinacotheca. The oicus he directs to be made of the same proportions as to length and breadth as the triclinium; that is, twice its width in length. If it was surrounded by a simple row of columns, it was called Corinthian; but if constructed of two orders, the upper closed with windows, it was termed Egyptian, and appeared like a basilica. In either case the area included within the peristyle was left uncovered for the admission of light.

There were also Cyzicenous oici, planned to open towards the north, with a view of the viridium, or conservatory: they were made sufficiently long and broad to admit two triclinia opposite each other, and also commanding by windows a view of the garden.

Strangers did not uninvited go into the cubiculum, triclinium, bath, or other apartments appropriated to the

---

[1] Atrium is supposed to be the term for the whole area included within the four walls of this part of the house.

private and particular uses of the master of the house[1] and his family; a part of the building which would by eminence be called the oicos, or house: but any who had business to transact might enter the vestibulum, cavædium, or peristyle. To people of inferior condition, who had no clients, the vestibulum, tablina, or atrium, were unnecessary. Dealers in the produce of the country required shops, cellars, and store-houses within; constructed rather with reference to the preservation of the goods to be placed therein than elegance of proportion. But to public characters, magistrates, who by their office had to decide upon the affairs of their countrymen, a vestibulum, a lofty atrium, with an ample peristyle, or portico and ambulatories, were requisite, in conformity with their rank and dignity; as well as libraries, pinacotheca, and basilica: but our author may be here supposed to allude to the more sumptuous palaces of the senators of Rome.

In the city, the atrium is placed near the entrance; in the country, the peristyle occupied that situation, and the atrium was within.

In the arrangement of the Greek house there was no atrium. It was entered through a passage, or thyroreion, which had gates outwards and inwards, immediately to a peristyle. On either side of the entrance was the stable, and porter's apartments. The peristyle occupied only three sides: on the fourth were two antæ, at an ample distance asunder, with a connecting archi-

[1] He snapped his fingers when he wanted a servant. The modern Greeks and Turks clap their hands.

trave: two thirds of their distance apart was the depth, and this was called the prostas, or parastas. Within was the great oicos, in which the family resided: on the right and left of the parastas were the cubicula; of which one was called thalamus, the other amphithalamus. Around under the portico, were the commonly used triclinia, cubicula, and cella familiarica.

KITCHEN IN THE HOUSE OF ACTÆON.

HOUSES.

In the unvarying climate of the south of Italy, that necessity for providing against the vicissitude of seasons and severity of winter, which we find in less favoured latitudes, does not exist. Good foundations and stout walls were not considered of essential consequence, where the skill of the architect was rather directed to the exclusion of heat than precaution against the less mild months of the year. Hence we find scarcely a house in the whole city of Pompeii, of which the walls are not considerably indebted for their durability to the plaster with which they are covered. Ill built, of the worst brick and rubble work, with mortar, generally, but insufficiently mixed, their thickness in few instances appears adequate to the service they were intended to perform.

The plaster is, however, sometimes very excellent, and appears to have been used precisely in the manner prescribed by Vitruvius, who directs that, after the first rough coat was applied, a second was to be added, of arenatum, composed principally of sand and lime;[1] this was afterwards to be covered with marmoratum, in the composition of which the place of the sand of the arenatum was supplied by pounded marble.

The last coat at Pompeii was put on very thin, and seems to have been well worked and rubbed upon the rough exterior of the arenatum, until a perfectly level, smooth, and, at length, polished surface, was obtained, nearly as hard as marble. While the last coat was still wet the colours were laid on, and, so done, becoming, according to Vitruvius, incorporated with the incrustation, were not liable to fade, but retained their full beauty and splendour to a great age. To be executed properly, three coats of arenatum, and as many of marmoratum, were used, which prevented the work cracking, and the surface might be polished so highly as to reflect objects.[2]

---

[1] Decomposed lava, or Vesuvian sand, is generally used in the arenatum, and first coats.

[2] The Doric columns at Corinth have been covered with a cement, of which little more was applied than was absorbed by the porous surface:

The smallest apartments were lined with this stucco, painted in the most brilliant and endless variety of colours, in compartments, simply tinted with a light ground, surrounded by an ornamental margin, and sometimes embellished with a single figure, or subject, in the centre, or at equal distances. The hand of the artist is everywhere visible, while a general acquaintance with the unrivalled taste of more ancient times is manifested in an elegance demanding and receiving our admiration.

These paintings are very frequently of history, but embrace every variety of subject, some of the most exquisite beauty. Greek artists seem to have been employed: indeed, native painters were few, while the former everywhere abounded; and their superiority in design must have always ensured them the preference.[1]

But it must not be expected that the paintings to be found in the excavated cities should throw equal light upon every branch of that art, carried by the ancients to so high a degree of perfection, and that in every depart-

---

those of Pæstum were also covered with a thicker coat. At Pompeii, the absorbent texture of the volcanic stone is peculiarly adapted to receive this, which, improving the appearance, at the same time retards decomposition. The quantity of mortar increased with the decline of art. None is found in the earliest Greek works, where cramps and tenons of wood, iron, and bronze were employed. Little, comparatively, was used in good Roman work, while the lower Greek wall was half made up of it. But the invention of the arch increased its use, with the employment of materials of smaller dimensions in the construction of edifices greater in extent than any contemplated by the ancients.

[1] Few artists or painters were Romans; and of poets, only Julius Cæsar, Tibullus, and Lucretius.

ment we are to find ourselves justified in the eulogiums universally bestowed upon their great masters.

Pompeii was but a small town, and, in all probability, contained no celebrated specimen of any artist of consequence; and if by chance any esteemed work had been included within the walls at the period of its destruction, can we imagine that an excavation of ten or twelve, at most twenty feet, would have proved an obstacle insurmountable to its recovery?

In grandeur and facility of drawing they warrant all that can be said in their praise: with that feeling for simplicity which distinguishes the ancients from the moderns, many are quite in the taste of the finest bas reliefs, which, like their tragedies, admitted no under-plot to heighten or embarrass. In colouring they are said to be deficient, want transparency in the shadows, exhibit little knowledge of *chiar' oscuro*, each figure has its own light and shade, while none are obscured by the interposition of its neighbour. But if we are called upon to make allowances in some of these points for the lapse of centuries, when viewing the works of a later age; how much more indulgence may be claimed, where two thousand years might reasonably have been expected to leave no traces at all![1]

At the same time it must be admitted, that having attained a degree of perfection acknowledged to be of the highest order of art, and found certain forms beyond which human genius could not imagine, the ancients

[1] Where the outer coat has peeled off, it is frequently seen that the picture has been painted upon a ground of green or red.

seem to have considered that all invention was to cease; the beautiful declared in one shape, few dared search its attainment in another; and subsequent professors became, as in Egypt,[1] a race of mere tradesmen; as imitators, degenerating, of course, in an inverse ratio, to their distance from the time of the great artists, whose works they studied with less skill than devotion, often copying as beautiful, and considering to be derived from excess of genius, even their faults and errors.

With reference to the architectural subjects, many are continually found in which it is easy to trace the true principles of perspective; but they are rather indicated than minutely expressed, or accurately displayed; whereas, in most instances, a total want of the knowledge of this art is but too evident.

A Roman, from the testimony of Pliny,[2] was the inventor of that peculiar style of profuse architectural decoration common at Pompeii; and which seems to have been so generally admired, that it became a fashion, to the exclusion of the more substantial style it superseded,[3] to the great annoyance of Vitruvius, whose censure it seems to have awakened. That architect inveighed in vain against the custom of thus adorning the walls of houses with representations, which he declares not to interest the mind: he liked not the sub-

---

[1] "Pictura quoque non alium exitum fecit, postquam Ægyptiorum audacia tam magnæ artis compendiariam invenit."—PETRON.

[2] I, 35-6.

[3] This art obtained the name of ropography; its professors, ropographers, or twig-painters.—SUIDAS.

stitution of the slender reed, or candelabra-form pillar, in the place of the more regular but massive column; nor foliaged twists for the formal pediment; and, forgetting the Corinthian capital, could not approve of that mixture of foliage and volutes with semi-animals, the remains of which are among the most admired fragments of architectural antiquity.

The walls of the houses are also decorated with painted imitations of variegated marbles, perhaps once a sort of scagliola. Of the real material, few blocks are found, except in public buildings, or monuments. In this the Pompeians imitated the more costly reality of the Romans, who inserted in their walls pieces, or slabs, of the most rare and valuable marbles: the undulated Thasian, or Carystian; the vermiculated Phrygian, spotted with the blood of Atys; the Numidian conglomerate.[1]

But the real colours of the marbles were not sufficiently splendid: art was employed to give them tints they possessed not naturally. The Numidian and Synnadic were used as thresholds, and a method was discovered of veining slabs with gold; until at length leaves of this metal were introduced in profusion, covering the beams, walls, and even roofs of the houses.[2]

[1] Bergier explains "ovatus" gilded. It was infinitely more beautiful,—a fine conglomerate.

[2] The taste of the Romans, in preferring the coloured marbles, has been censured, and the works of the Greeks referred to as purer models for imitation. The fact, however, is, that no nation ever exhibited a greater passion for gaudy colours, with which, in the absence of the rarer marbles, they covered the surface of the beautiful pentelic. Blue marble is mixed with white in one of their best examples, the temple of Minerva Polias, at Athens; while even their statues were seldom left colourless.

The floors, also, were covered with cement, in which, while yet unset, small pieces of marble, or coloured stones, were imbedded at intervals, forming various patterns of geometrical figures, symmetrically disposed:[1] but this was the practice only in apartments of inferior consequence; for in the best rooms mosaic was used, with ornamented margins, and a device, or figure, in the centre.[2] Some fine specimens of this work are frequently found; but the best and most perfect have been removed to the royal museum at Naples, where many of them form the actual floors of the rooms in which the more portable remains of this city are deposited for public inspection.

A valuable memoir[3] upon the colours used in the paintings of the ancients has been drawn up by Sir Humphry Davy. M. Chaptal[4] has also published a paper upon seven colours found in a shop at Pompeii.

Sir H. Davy considers the Greek and Roman painters to have been possessed of almost all the colours used by the great artists of the Italian school at the period of the revival of the arts in Italy, with an advantage of two, not known to the latter: the Egyptian or Vestorian azure, and the Tyrian or marine purple. The azure, with the red and yellow ochres, and the blacks, are those which appear to have undergone the least change in the frescos. The vermilion is darker: the greens in

---

[1] Pounded tile was put upon the stucco in the more ordinary rooms.
[2] The remains of a carpet were in one instance found.
[3] Printed in the 'Phil. Trans.,' 1815.
[4] 70th vol. of 'Ann. de Chim.'

general dull: but the massicot and orpiment are the least permanent amongst the mineral pigments employed by the ancients.

It is the opinion of Sir Humphry, that the ancient painters, like the best masters of the Roman and Venetian schools, were sparing in the use of the more florid colours, and produced their effects, like them, by contrast and tone; admitting little more than the red and yellow ochres, black and white, in their best works: but gold was sometimes introduced, as in the early Italian school. The paintings upon the walls appear sometimes to have been varnished by an encaustic process; many specimens bearing a semi-polish, or gloss, to which water does not readily adhere. Rubbing will not detach the colour; which could have been washed with little damage, and none to the stucco, if revarnished.[1]

The doors, formed of wood, are never found complete; this material, being always reduced to carbon, retaining only the general form. Fir appears to have been much used. The doors revolved upon pivots,[2] and were fastened by bolts, which hung from chains. The windows were

[1] Vitruvius, 7—3, seems to intend that it should bear washing.

[2] The commentators have imagined the noise attending the opening of ancient doors to have been a necessary notice, given by the persons coming from within to the bystanders without, as they opened in that direction; but they might have observed, in the 'Bacchides,' 4, 7, 35, that the same followed upon entering the house. The wooden pivot was, as well as the socket wherein it revolved, an inverted cone; the former nearly cylindrical: this, when worn, sunk deeper, and, fitting tight, with the dryness of the wood, occasioned the creaking, which a little moisture would obviate. In 'Curculio,' the old woman, for that purpose, applies some water.

seldom glazed: they were closed at night by shutters, not too well put together; but the gaping chinks were covered with curtains.[1]

Of wood were also the bedsteads, though sometimes of iron: but beds were more generally made merely of carpets and vests, spread upon the ground.[2]

It does not enter within the plan of this work to give detailed accounts of every article of household furniture or convenience found at Pompeii: suffice it to say, that almost every variety is to be met with in the museum at Naples. Implements of silver, brass, stone, earthenware vases of all sizes, adapted to every use, whether sacred or profane; trumpets, bells, gridirons, colanders, saucepans, some lined with silver, kettles, ladles, moulds for jelly or pastry, urns for keeping water hot, upon the principle of the modern tea-urn, lanterns, with horn, spits; in short, almost every article of kitchen or other furniture now in use, except forks.

Chains, bolts, scourges, portable fire-places, with contrivances for heating water; dice (some said to be loaded); a complete toilet, with combs, thimbles, rings, paint, ear-rings, with pearls; pins for the hair; almonds, dates, nuts, figs, grapes, eggs, raisins, and chesnuts.[3]

[1] .... "claude fenestras
Vela tegant rimas, junge ostia."—JUVENAL.

[2] "Lodiculum in pavimento diligenter extende."—JUV.
Et multa passim exempla. It is the present custom in Turkey.

[3] The two latter are said to be not ripe so early in the year as the date assigned to the destruction of the city. A new reading has therefore been invented for the manuscripts. An early season might have been conjectured, or a superior method of preserving them.

The name of the owner or occupier is constantly found upon the door-post:

SABINVM·ET·RVFVM A·D·R·P·VNENTINVS·CVM
DISCENTES·SVOS·ROG

A C V L I I L O JV
AEDILYS·FAMILIA·GLADIATORIA·POMPEIS
PR·K·IVNIAS·VENATIO·ET·VELA·ERVNT
VETTIVM·AED

C·IVLIVM·POLYBIVM
II VIR·MVLIONES·ROG

CERIVM·ET·SABINVM
IIVIR·ED·O·V·

The precise construction of these inscriptions is still open to the conjectures of the learned. They certainly intimate the connection between the occupier and his patron, whose name is always most conspicuous. In the first, Unentinus, with his disciples, places his house under the protection of Sabinus and Rufus, who were probably Romans. The second has been engraved upon an old, worn-out inscription, and gives notice of a gladiatorial combat. In the next, Muliones claims the patronage of Julius Polybius, a duumvir; and the contractions of the last line may be read, "ædem orat ut faveat."

The method of watering the town will be found to have been by a general distribution of fountains, and we may recollect that Cato forbade any individual having the public water laid on to his house. Like all the early laws intended to restrain the progress of luxury, this was of course soon given up. Besides the general supply, each individual seems to have made himself a tank for preserving the rain water.

PLATE XX.

The villa Suburbana.[1] Between the mass of building and the more distant bank runs the Street of the Tombs. Like the houses of the east, this presents nothing to the road but a bare wall; the windows being all towards the garden. The bath will be observed, and the remains of the six columns of the ædiculum. Of the ambulatory, much restored, only two sides remain; over it was the terrace, with a summer-house at each of the hither corners. The arch to the left leads to the cellar where the skeletons of the family alluded to (page 65,) were found.

PLATE XXI.

Triangular room and bath in the villa Suburbana.
To render this view more explanatory, the two columns to the right, which now only partly exist, are carried up to their capitals. The bath appears behind the centre columns.

[1] For the plan, see Plate II.

POMPEII.

VIEW OF THE VILLA SUBURBANA.

POMPEII.

Engraved by Chas. Heath.

POMPEII.

MEETING OF TWO STREETS IN TRIVIIS, AT THE HOUSE OF PANSA.

POMPEII.

PLATE XXII.

View of the junction in triviis of two streets at the house of Pansa. At the point whence they diverge is a fountain, upon the back of which is a representation of an eagle seizing a hare. A regular supply is of the last importance to the inhabitants of a warm climate, where water is scarce; and to this day, in Turkey, the erection of fountains by the road-side for the convenience and refreshment of the traveller, is looked upon as a work of pious benevolence.[1] We may imagine that he who committed wilful depredation, or in any way injured them, would be considered by such conduct in the greatest degree deserving more than human punishment. Upon each of the acroteria of the temple of Nemesis at Rhamnus is a representation of a gryphon pouncing upon a hart; thus intimating that the retributive justice of that goddess overtook even the fleetest of animals. The hare and eagle may be considered a parallel allegory, and thus an emblem of divine vengeance exhibited; as a warning to those whom the ordinary principles of rectitude could not restrain.

PLATE XXIII.

View in the house of the Vestals.

The great court of this house, which backed against the city walls, must have been very handsome, as will be imagined from the remaining columns of its peristyle, or inner area. The middle of the three doors seen at

---

[1] We find Agrippa thus employed himself in ancient Rome.

the farther end, is of the passage connecting this with the first court, where was the entrance from the street seen on the left. Into the same street was also a way through a room, upon the wall of which the spectator is supposed to stand. Castel-a-mare and the island Rivegliano are seen in the distance, bounded by Mount Lactarius, ending to the right in the promontory of Minerva.

The tiled covering upon these walls is modern, for the purpose of preserving them.

PLATE XXIV.

This probably represents a scene in a play. The artist seems to have possessed considerable knowledge of perspective, and has also displayed some acquaintance with architectural composition; but the whole is too precisely represented in the engraving. In the original, all the ornamented parts are undetermined in form, though not in character; the figures, also, are sketches. The border is from a room; the ground yellow, flowers alternately green and red.

PLATE XXV.

View in the court of a house near the foregoing: the space within the columns was open; around is a gutter for conveying away the water which fell from the roof. At the farther end is seen a niche: the wall is painted, and this part was, probably, roofed. The door to the right of the niche is to the room where were found

POMPEII.

PAINTING IN THE HOUSE CALLED THE VESTALS.

POMPEII.

Engraved by Chas. Heath.

POMPEII.

PICTURES AND ORNAMENTS

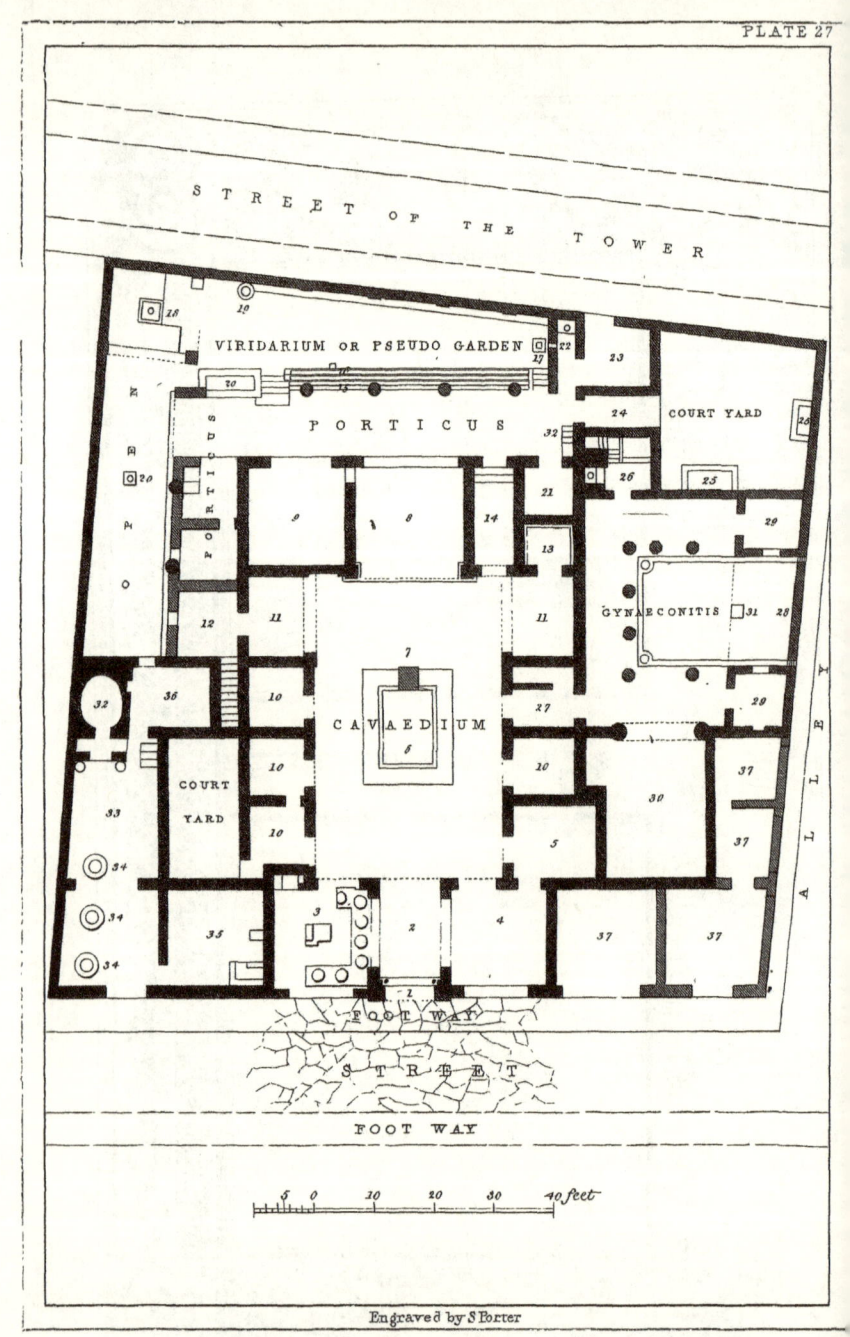

POMPEII.

PLAN OF THE HOUSE OF SALLUST CALLED OF ACTAEON.

the surgical instruments whence the house obtained its name. To the left, but out of the picture, was the entrance through the first court. There was also a communication with a parallel street, to the right of the view, but not seen. The unfluted portions of the columns are painted blue; the dwarf walls between, red. The tiles upon the walls are modern.

PLATE XXVI.

Outlines of two paintings upon a wall. They are surrounded by ornaments from various quarters; that in the centre had a mirror.
They are principally from the house of the Vestals.

PLATE XXVII.

Plan of the house of Sallust:

C · SALLVSTIVM ·

Sallust was, perhaps, only the patron of its occupier; it has obtained the name of Actæon from a picture of Diana and Actæon, which still adorns the inner court.
It is built irregularly, and communicates with two streets.
1. The principal entrance, paved with mosaic.
2. The vestibulum, or passage to the cavædium.
3. A shop, with a counter; round the front and sides were jars, probably for wine or oil.

4. Another apartment, for the purpose of traffic. It communicates with the cavædium by the apartment (5).
6. Compluvium, or shallow cistern, for collecting the water which fell through the roof. In it was a bronze stag.
7. Altar for the household god.
8. Tablinum, with an inner room (9). They were both separated from the garden by wide windows upon a dwarf wall. The latter was probably triclinium, or cubiculum,[1] and is adorned with representations of scenic masks. A compartment opposite the window is given in Plate xxxiii. The stucco floor imitated a white breccia.
10. Cella familiaria: bed-chambers not ten feet square.
11. Alæ. One of these opened into the room (12), from which was a staircase to the upper apartments.
13. Lararium, or pinacotheca.
14. Fauces, or passage to the viridarium, pseudo-garden, or green-house, the floor of which was three feet above the porticus. Two flights of steps conducted to the higher level; between them were the dwarf walls (15), and an inner wall, formed to contain earth for plants. Between the two was a gutter to receive the water from the roof. The back wall is painted with shrubs, birds, &c. At one end was a tank (17). At the other the triclinium (18); with the pedestal for the table. This latter part was covered over.
19. Fountain.
20. Another tank. The portico originally returned on this side, but is now filled in with apartments built at a subsequent period.
21. Cubiculum.
22. Privy.
23. Back entrance.
24. Passage to a court yard.
25. Places for ashes.

[1] "In cornu porticûs amplissimum cubiculum a triclinio cucurrit." Petron.

26. Kitchen, and privy for the women's apartments. Of this a view is given as the foregoing head-piece. On the right of the way up stairs is the hearth for cooking, separated therefrom by wooden ballusters, which do not remain. On the other side is an arched recess, about three feet deep; a conveniency, according to modern, at least English ideas, most inconveniently situated. The wood work of the seat is gone: the marks for the hinges, and fastening to the door, may be observed.[1]

It would appear, that in ancient, as in modern Italy and Greece, a proximity between the ultimate receptacle of the aliments and their place of preparation was considered desirable.[2]

In ancient Rome were 144 public cloacinæ; also the public walk, with the Sellæ Patroclianæ: perhaps something of this sort remains to be found at Pompeii, where few houses can boast the possession of such convenience at all: but the Lasana were portable.[2]

27. Entrance from the cavædium to a third court, perhaps the Gynæconitis, or women's apartments, with a porticus; the columns are octangular, painted red. Between these the floor was in patterns of mosaic.

28. Against the wall is a picture of Diana, bathing, and Actæon, with horns, chased by his own hounds. In other parts appear Europa, Helle, Phrixus.

29. Small apartments, or cubicula. One of them is highly finished, with delicate painting, and pavement, dado, &c. of different coloured marbles. On one side is Mars and Venus: again, Cupid playing with his arms; on another, a recess for Penates, or Lares. They are entered from the portico. The other openings,

---

[1] Petronius might well say, "Quam bene olere qui in culinâ habitant." If this had been the plan of Plautus' kitchen, we should not doubt the angle alluded to in the Persa, where the pretended Virgo, to give an idea of her low birth, says she was born: "Ut mater dixit, in culinâ, in angulo ad lævam manum."

[2] Hor., Sat. I, 6, 109.

opposite each other, are windows: the intermediate space was roofed.
30. Large apartment for the women.
31. Pedestal, or altar.
32. Oven.
33. Bakehouse.
34. Mills for grinding the corn.
35. Contiguous apartment.
36. Room perhaps for charcoal.
37. Shops, &c.

PLATE XXVIII.

Atrium, or cavædium, of the foregoing house. In the centre is the compluvium and altar of the domestic divinity; beyond which is the tablinum, separated by a dwarf wall from the green-house, or viridarium. The Ionic columns for the support of the roof of the porticus of this are seen, and its painted wall beyond. Upon the dwarf wall was constructed the large window. To the right is the communicating passage, called fauces: right and left the alæ, or conversation recesses, which probably had divans. The door-ways of the apartments surrounding the cavædium are also seen on each side; their painted walls, and that of the cavædium itself, may be observed, imitating slabs of marble. The floor was red cement, with bits of white stone imbedded. A false door appears to the left of the tablinum, to correspond with the fauces: it may hence be conjectured that the doors were sometimes thus painted.[1] Vitruvius directs that the opening for the tablinum should be 1-8th in height more than the width; about the proportion here given. The tiled tops to the walls are modern.

[1] See Plate XXXI.

Engraved by Chas Heath.

POMPEII.

HOUSE (CALLED) OF ACTAEON.

PLATE 22.

POMPEII

Engraved by H. Moses.

PLATE XXIX.

Restored Atrium of the house of Sallust, or Actæon.

By comparing this with the preceding view of the room in its present state, it will be seen how far the restoration is authorised. The compluvium and impluvium will be observed. Near the latter is a contrivance for heating water, found in this house, but now in the Royal Museum. The lower square part is of bronze, lined with iron, and held the charcoal fire. The round perforation in the bottom probably had a grating, to quicken the heat by the passage of air. Over this, the three eagles were to support a kettle. The semicircular piece on which they are placed was hollow, and through it ran the heated water, (to a cock on the left,) from the reservoir, of which the lid is open. The whole was moveable.

The triclinium, opening upon the pseudo-garden, is opposite the spectator. The fauces on the right form the regular communication with the latter, and a false door on the other side is made to correspond. The alæ, or exedra, will be observed on the right and left. The openings were, perhaps, only covered with curtains; in Greek, according to Pollux, called *parapetasma;* commonly white, but sometimes poikile, or painted; as was, probably, that to the fauces, like the false door. In the palatial commotions, Claudius hid himself "inter prætenta foribus vela;" as did Heliogabalus, on a like occasion.—SUETONIUS—LAMPRIDIUS.

The couches were spread with carpets, as were also the floors of the rooms, in the modern Turkish manner.

PLATE XXX.

Side of an apartment in the foregoing house.
The sickle-form ornaments at the upper part afford the best possible explanation of the harpaginetuli of Vitruvius.

PLATE XXXI.

1. A sacrifice upon the blank door, see Plate xxviii. Under it is a serpent, the genius of the place.[1] The priest covered his head during sacrifice. He pours the contents of the patera upon the tripod. Opposite him is a young man, who performs upon the double flute; his foot is upon a scabillum, which was thus played upon by the Tibicina. On each side are two assistants, dressed alike: their robes are white; a double narrow red stripe runs down the front of the tunic, of which colour is also the piece of drapery to each. In one hand they each hold a vase, in shape of a horn, from which they pour liquor into a patera.[2]
2. From a wall, painted.
3. Cymatium of terra cotta, with scenic masks, or persona, perforated to spout the water from the roof.
4. Cornice, &c., with lions' heads for a similar purpose.
5, 6, 7, are also painted upon various walls.

[1] Servius, Æneid, v, 84.

[2] "Funde merum genio."—Pers., ii, 3.

"Floribus et vino genium memorem brevis ævi."
                                        Hor., *Epist.*

POMPEII.

HOUSE OF ACTÆON SIDE OF A ROOM

POMPEII.

PAINTING TILES AND ORNAMENTS IN THE HOUSE OF ACTAEON

POMPEII.

PSEUDO GARDEN AND TRICLINIUM HOUSE OF ACTÆON.

PLATE XXXII.

Pseudo-garden, or viridarium. The back wall is painted with pilasters, shrubs, and trellice-work; behind the columns, upon a double wall, were planted flowers and shrubs. The porticus on the right of the columns was covered over, and ranged in front of the tablinum; but the space between this and the painted wall upon a higher level was open, except the hither end, where a triclinium, somewhat similar to that of the Street of the Tombs, will be observed, with the trapezophoron, or pillar for supporting the table. The lower portions of the columns and pilasters were painted blue. Only two of the capitals now remain, two are restored for the purpose of making the view more explanatory.

The owner of this house seems to have made the most of the small proportion of outlet remaining to him; and as the building in this part was but one story high, the mode of decoration adopted, and mixture of painting with the reality of herbage, might have had a pleasing effect.

PLATE XXXIII.

Masks in the room of the house of Sallust, marked (9). The vast size of the ancient theatres rendered expedients necessary which are only resorted to in modern pantomime, where the painted face of the clown affords some likeness to two of those before us. The female characters acted by men must have been ill assisted by the other masks, of which the tragic intention is indicated by the cup and hellebore. The surrounding ornaments are copied from various parts of this house; the lower (6) is red and blue, upon grounds of pink and white.

PLATE XXXIV.

Plan of the house of Pansa.

This was a complete insula, surrounded by four streets, ambitus, or angiportus; but although thus completely separated from its neighbours, the whole does not seem to have been in the occupation of an individual.

Trade by the Romans was always considered degrading, particularly if not extensive;[1] they therefore employed their slaves, freed-men, or hirelings, to sell on their account. These were named institores, and termed inquilinus.[2]

---

[1] Cic., Off. I, iv, 2.
[2] Cataline calls Cicero "inquilinus civis," or a lodger.—Sall.

Engraved by Chas Heath.

POMPEII.

HOUSE OF ACTÆON. ORNAMENTS, PAINTING &c.—

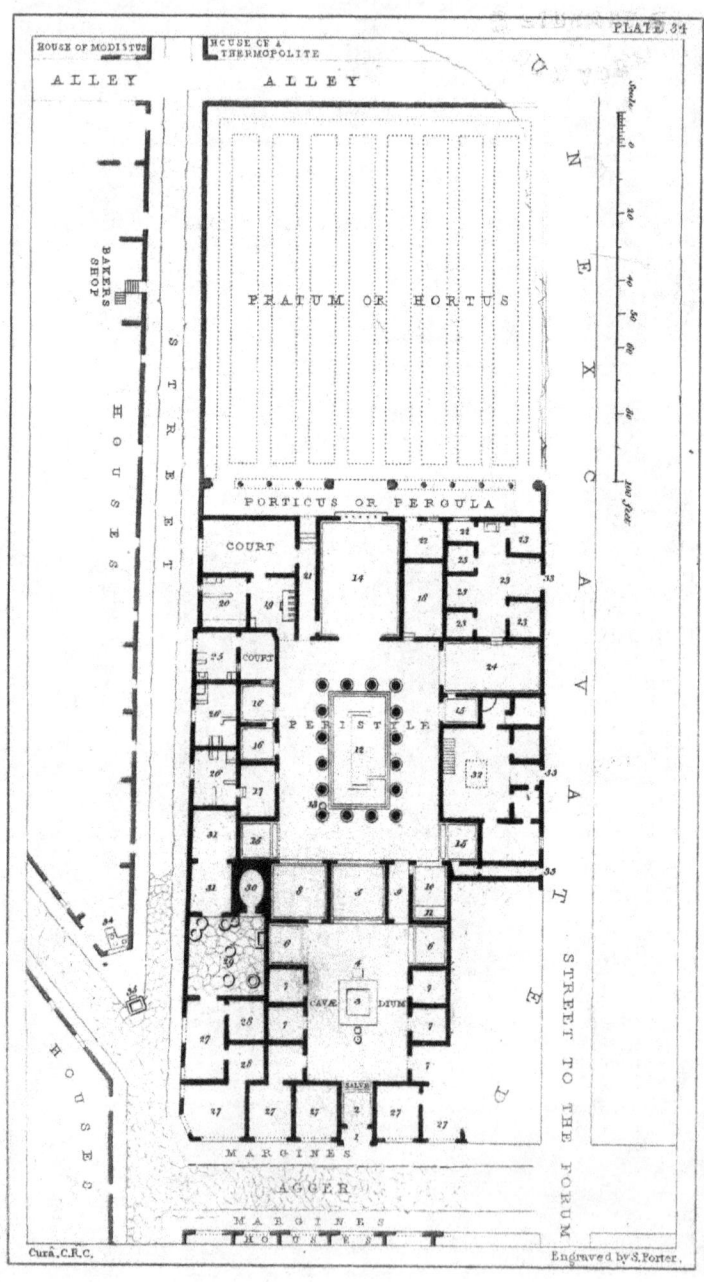

POMPEII.

PLAN OF THE HOUSE OF PANSA.

The practice of the owner may be compared to that of the proprietors of some of the great palaces of Italy; who, occupying themselves the best suite of rooms, let out to hire the lower apartments of their houses. So Pansa the dominus retaining the centre, seems to have let those rooms next the street to bakers and other tradesmen,[1] for whose traffic they were well situated.

1. Entrance, paved with mosaic. Macrobius, with Aulus Gellius, were of opinion that the vestibulum was the proper appellation for that part of the house between the entrance and first court; but Cæcilius Gallus, as quoted by Servius, declares it to be without the doors, though not in the street.
2. Vestibulum, paved also with mosaic. The ostiarius, or porter, stood here, for which office a chained slave[2] was usual, with a dog;[3] the latter sometimes only painted.

The word salve is no where shown; as illustrative it has been transferred from another house, where it occurs in a similar situation.

The cavædium contains in the centre the basin (3), or compluvium, formed to receive the water which fell from the roof, through an aperture left in the ceiling for the

---

[1] People sometimes let or sold their houses, retaining one of these.—PLAUT., Trinum, l. 2, 158.

"Posticulum hoc recepit cum ædis vendidit."

[2] Suetonius speaks of this as an antiquated custom.

[3] In Petronius is a dog, painted with "Cave canem:" over it was a cage, with a magpie, taught to salute those who entered with the word Χαιρε. Against the door-post was affixed a notice, that whoso without leave passed the threshold should be punished with 100 stripes. In the palace of Alcinöus, the dogs were of gold and silver. Dogs or lions were over the gates at Mycenæ, before the gates of Egyptian temples, and within the entrance to the infernal regions.

Before the triclinium was the servant who received and carried in messages, and showed in visitors.

admission of light to the rooms arranged around. This was called the impluvium.[1] Varro says, the cavædium was a room originally of common use, around which were cella, penaria, cubicula, and cœnacula.[2] It was the same as the atrium, which Festus puts in front of the house; and says, the rain collected from the surrounding roofs fell into it. The kitchen was therein, according to Servius; and the gods were there worshipped. Vitruvius teaches that cavædia were of five kinds: Tuscan, Corinthian, tetrastyle, displuviated, and testudinated.

One of the proportions of Vitruvius is,—the length to be once and half the breadth; here it is precisely so, 47 feet 4 inches by 31 feet 6 inches.

4. A pedestal, or altar, of the household god.
5. The tablinum, paved with mosaic. This was separated from the cavædium by an aulæum, or curtain like a drop scene. Next the inner court was sometimes, if not generally, a window,[3] occupying the whole side. In summer the tablinum was used as a dining-room.
6. Alæ. These recesses, surrounded on three sides by seats, are analogous to similar in the galleries of Turkish houses, with their divans. They were paved with mosaic. According to Vitruvius, when the length of the atrium is from 40 to 50 feet, they are to be two sevenths; a proportion which agrees precisely with

---

[1] It was sometimes a piscina, and contained fish.

"Ad januam venimus ubi canis catenarius tanto nos tumultu excepit ut Asclytus in piscinam cecidit."—PETRON.

[2] The compluvium seems sometimes to have been meant merely to collect the water, which was conveyed therefrom by a pipe into a reservoir below, where it was preserved for use.

[3] "Interea suspensa graves aulæa ruinas,
In patinam fecêre trahentia pulveris atri."
HOR., Sat. II, viii, 54.

Virgil speaks of them as purpurea and superba; and Pollux, as poikile.

these. The alæ did not reach to the ceiling, as their breadth and height were the same.[1]
7. Penaria, cellæ domesticæ, or cubicula. These were domestic apartments.
8. Probably pinacotheca, or apartments for pictures, books, &c.
9. Fauces, or communicating passage between the outer and inner division of the house.
10. Cubiculum. Its use cannot be doubted, as it contains a bedstead, which fills up the whole width of the farther end.

The Peristyle, according to Vitruvius, should have in length $1\frac{1}{2}$ its breadth; precisely the proportion of the example before us. The columns are to be as high as the dimension from their front to the wall.

This is presumed to have been the oicus of Vitruvius; if so, it was of the description termed Egyptian, since the porticus surrounding it had two orders of columns.

The water from the eaves[2] fell into a channel which ran close to the bases of the columns, and was conveyed into a deep basin in the centre (12). The sides of this were painted with representations of reeds and aquatic plants: it possibly contained fish. Against one of the columns was a puteal over a tank (13).
14. The triclinium; raised two steps from the peristyle, and separated from the garden by a large window. In this room company was received, and chairs placed for their accommodation.[3]

---

[1] Gloss. vet. Ala σχολη, εξεδρα.

[2] In the 'Orestes' of Euripides, on the murder of Helen, the Phrygian attendant escaped through this aperture. The order was Doric.

"Κεδρωτα πασταδων υπερ
τερεμνα δορικας τε τριγλυφας."

[3] The Greek and Roman ladies sat in the triclinium, while the men reclined.—VAL. MAX., ii, 1. Hence, for a lectisternium, they prepared lecti for the gods, while the goddesses were placed in chairs.—PLINY, viii, 21.

15. Exedra.

In the note to the alæ, it will be seen that they were analogous to the exedra.

The siesta was taken in the exedra. They were also for conversation.[1]

16. Cellæ familiaricæ, or family chambers. These two were very beautifully finished, and paved with mosiac: advantages the more common (marked 17) did not possess. One had a window looking into the small court.

18. Lararium, or armarium, the receptacle for the more revered and favorite gods.[2]

19. Kitchin, containing stoves. It opened into a court, and had an inner room (20), in which were dwarf walls, to arrange oil jars.

21. Fauces, conducting to the garden. A pergula or portico for training vines and creepers ranged along the back front of the house, before the windows of the triclinium.

22. These two rooms opening into the pergula are presumed to be cubicula.

23. The apartments thus marked seem to have constituted a distinct portion of the house, and communicated with the street by a separate door. That they were included in Pansa's establishment may be inferred from their being connected with the peristyle by the large apartment (24). The greater part of this had been very recently excavated: amongst other matters were found four skeletons of females, marked by their gold ear-rings; also a candelabrum, two vases, a fine marble head of a fawn, gold bracelets, rings with engraved

---

[1] "In eam exedram venisse in qua Crassus lectulo posito recubuisset."—Cic., de Orat., 3.

[2] "In angulo porticus grande armarium vidi in cujus ædicula erant Lares argentei positi."—Petron.

The Lararium held also statues of persons whose characters were held in estimation by the owner of the house, as Virgil, Cicero.—Lampridius.

stones, 32 pieces of small silver coin, with various other articles.

25, 26. Shops. They appear, by the remains of their staircases seen on the sides, to have had apartments above. In them are dwarf walls, to range oil jars and other goods against: 25 had a door and a window into the small court, which lighted a room in Pansa's house.

27. Are different shops. One is of a baker; to it are annexed all the necessary conveniences.

28. Apotheca, or store-rooms.

29. The bakehouse, containing the oven[1] (30), three mills, a kneading-bowl, &c. It is paved with volcanic stone, in polygonal shapes.

31. Here was deposited the stock of wood and charcoal.

32. Seems to have been almost a distinct dwelling. Two of the apartments had windows to the street, which runs southward to the Forum.

33. Entrances from this street to the house of Pansa.

34. Oinopolium, or Thermopolium. Shop of a seller of warm and sweet drinks: the ascent to the upper story was by fifteen steps. Plautus treats the frequenters of these places as drunkards. Epicures resorted to them for vomits,[2] which were considered luxuries. Vitellius by such means contrived to sup through the whole night. Saccharine matter was kept candied for solution in warm water.[3] Stewed meat was also here sold.

35. Fountain.

It will be seen that the streets around the house of Pansa are paved, like the rest of the city, with volcanic stone, in polygonal shapes. The margines, or foot paces, are raised irregularly, not to say incommodiously. It will

[1] Plate XXXVIII.

[2] The love of this remedy is remarkable in the existing lower class of Neapolitans of the present day.

[3] PLINY, xxiii, 1.

be also observed, that no fire-place exists, nor do any flues remain, by which the house could have been warmed by means of a stove, præfurnium, or hypocaust:[1] for this purpose, in all probability, only braziers were used, with charcoal, as they are frequently found.

PLATE XXXV.

Entrance to the house of Pansa. The Corinthian pilasters are of stone, without cement: behind them was a space before the door. This was the vestibulum, which was frequently adorned with columns,[2] and the pavement covered with coloured chalks, or pigments; but its exposed situation rendered some precaution necessary against the committing of nuisance.[3]
The columns of the inner peristyle are seen. Upon the side of the entrance is inscribed,

PANSAM·AED
PARATVS·ROG

Pansam ædem Paratus rogat ut faveat.[4]

[1] The Roman remains in England show this method of warming houses to have been common in a colder climate and later age.

[2] "Viden' vestibulum ante ædis hoc? Jussin' columnis dejicier operas arenarum et in splendorem dari bullas has foribus nostris."—PLAUTUS.

[3] "Pinge humum consperge ante ædis."—See the 'Stichus' of Plautus, act i, scene 3.

[4] If the inscription is to be thus read, we may presume Pansa to have been the dominus, and Paratus the keeper of the shop to the right of the door. Or was Paratus the owner of the whole insula, and Pansa his patron at Rome?

POMPEII.

ENTRANCE TO THE HOUSE OF PANSA.

POMPEII.

PERISTYLE OR INNER COURT OF THE HOUSE OF PANSA.

POMPEII.

RESTORATION OF THE ATRIUM IN THE HOUSE OF PANSA.

PLATE XXXVI.

Peristyle, or inner court of the house of Pansa. The columns were originally formed in lava, of the Ionic order: their flutings had subsequently been changed to Doric by means of plaster, and painted. The puteal is here seen, adjoining the nearest column.

PLATE XXXVII.

An attempt to explain the general arrangement of the cavædium in Pansa's house, with the nature of its ceiling, impluvium, and compluvium.

By a reference to the plan, it will be seen that the first two doors on each side are to the rooms marked thereon (7). Next come the alæ. The centre is occupied by the tablinum, having on the right the fauces, or passage through to the inner court. On the left, the pinacotheca; and through this latter are seen the doors to the rooms (16, 17). Beyond the tablinum are the columns of the peristyle, and the basin occupying its centre. In the distance, the triclinium and pergula, opening upon the garden.

In warm weather, the house was perhaps thus open to view through its whole extent; but the tablinum was sometimes separated from the peristyle by a window; and, when the aulæum was drawn or let down, formed a separate apartment.¹

The cavædium seems to have been lighted at night by a lamp, which served for all the surrounding apartments:

> "Abimus omnes cubitum condormivimus
> Lucernam forte oblitus fueram extinguere."¹

Around the room, upon the pedestals, are placed six of nine Muses, found painted in a house in this city. They are marked, beginning at the left, Melpomene, Erato, Thalia, Calliope, Terpsichore, Polymnia.

PLATE XXXVIII.

The bakehouse attached to the house of Pansa. Amongst the various articles found, and now preserved in the Royal Museum, is a loaf of bread, eight inches diameter: upon the top is,

SILIGO · CRANII
E · CICER

Siligo was a white, but little nutritive flour, although a better sort;³ a mixture of vetch was probably indicated by cicer, while Ranius declared the baker's name.

---

[1] In the 'Bacchides' of Plautus, the old man, opening the street door, sees his son feasting in the triclinium.

[2] Plaut., Mostell., ii, 2, 55.

[3] "Malum panem etiam tenerum tibi et siligineum fames reddit."— Seneca, Lett. 123.

POMPEII.

OVEN AND MILLS IN THE HOUSE OF PANSA.

Over the oven of Pansa was the baker's sign, painted a deep red,[1] and motto,

"Hic habitat felicitas."

The mills are of dark volcanic stone, very rough, and full of leucites. The upper portion, shaped in the inside, as well as the exterior, like an hourglass, seems to have been moved by a lever, inserted through the square aperture, and fastened by a cross pin, for which the hole may be observed. This is removed in one to show the conical piece whereon the moveable part turned, with another square sinking on its apex; probably to let something in for the purpose of fastening the lever, so as to keep all in its place. Over the top, where the corn was put in, is generally about two feet six inches; the flour fell around on the lower cylinder; two of these were within sixteen inches of the wall: consequently the lever could not have completed the circle.

Beyond the mill, in the corner, is a bowl for holding the water jar: to the right of this a bin, sunk below the floor, six feet long.

This room was coved.

---

[1] "Ruber porrectus."—HOR.

"Membra genitalia apud veteres præcipue colebantur quoniam ad generationem necessaria sunt; et per ea species animantium conservantur et propagantur; et abundantiæ et fœcunditatis signa sunt et præses credebantur incrementis frugum et pecudum.

". . . . . æstate frequentor Spicis."—EP. 85, in Pr.

PLATE XXXIX.

View of the cavædium of the house, s.w. of the basilica. It is of the species termed by Vitruvius tetrastyle: the columns are of brick, plastered.[1] (See plan of the Forum, 36.) This and the adjoining house were excavated by the French General Championet. The entrance is to the left in the view. The floors are paved with mosaic.

PLATE XL.

Side of a room.

PLATE XLI.

Side of a room.
The designs of this and the foregoing are made out more by variety of colours than line; the latter only is here attempted. They consequently offer but inadequate representations of the originals.

---

[1] Crassus, the orator, was the first, 662 U.C., who introduced columns of foreign materials: he placed four of Hymettian marble in his atrium, twelve feet high. It was then considered a shameful piece of luxury; though, in a short time, no house of any consequence was without this sort of decoration.

POMPEII.

TETRASTYLE CAVÆDIUM IN THE HOUSE SOUTH OF THE BASILICA.

Engraved by Cha. Heath.

POMPEII.

SIDE OF A ROOM.

POMPEII.

SIDE OF A ROOM.

POMPEII.

PICTURE FROM THE EXCAVATION OF QUEEN CAROLINE.

PLATE XLII.

In the year 1813, Queen Caroline instituted an excavation in the street which runs from the south-east angle of the Forum towards the theatre. On removing the new soil, about eighteen inches in thickness, a skeleton was discovered, scarcely covered with the volcanic matter, being ten feet above the ancient pavement. This individual had secured 360 silver, 42 bronze, and 8 small imperial gold coins,[1] which were found with the skeleton, wrapped in a cloth.

The pictures represented in the present and following plates are from this excavation; but the frequent wettings they have undergone, to freshen the colours for the observation of the curious, have loosened great part of the fresco from the wall, until few traces remain for future revival. In the first, a male figure, whose head is surrounded with rays, reclines upon a seat. Before him appears a female, bearing a wand and purple peplum. Between them is Hymen, whose head is encircled with a wreath; a torch in one hand, in the other a branch of palm. It would be difficult to say precisely what persons the painter has here intended to represent. Lucian, in the dialogue between Venus and Diana, describes Endymion as sleeping upon a rock, over which his chlamys was spread, (here crimson, lined with blue;) in his left hand holding his spears, which almost escape his careless grasp.

---

[1] It is remarkable, that many skeletons are found out of doors, some feet above the ancient level; from which it would appear, that they had struggled some time before exhaustion.

In this excavation is a semicircular triclinium, or stibadium, in the open air, with a water-course around it. Cicero calls this a sigma, from its semi-lunar form.

In one of the pictures found at Herculaneum, a figure, answering to the description of Lucian, is seen sleeping, his right hand holding two spears: Diana, half draped, approaches, led by Cupid. The general arrangement of the subject alluded to, as well as the attitudes, bears a strong resemblance to the picture before us; but here the male figure, awake, holds the spears in his left hand. Diana is represented as by Propertius,

> "Nudus et Endymion Phœbi cepisse sororem
> Dicitur, et nudæ concubuisse deæ."

The palm branch is possibly symbolic of the victory of Cupid over the goddess of chastity. But the rays round the head? Was it Venus and Adonis? who was the same as the Sun, according to Macrobius, Sat. I, 21.

The ornaments arranged around the subject are from various houses. The design of the capitals, from an entrance, must be considered tasteful. The ornament between them is from a tomb.

PLATE XLIII.

This, without doubt, represents Perseus, after having liberated Andromeda, and petrified the sea-monster, to which she had been exposed. The wings upon his head and feet; the head of the Gorgon Medusa, held behind him, lest by its view the beholder should be turned to stone; the harpe, or two-pointed, scythe-like, adamantine sword, he received from Vulcan,[1] all clearly point out the son of Jupiter and Danaë.

[1] From Eratosthenes, or Mercury, according to Apollonius. Hesiod calls it αορ; Æschylus and Apollodorus, αρπη.

PLATE 43.

Engraved by Chas Heath.

POMPEII.

PAINTING.

The first care of Andromeda seems very properly to have been the toilet, since it was agreed she was not exposed in full dress. She wears a pink or white tunic, with a blue peplum.

The border is from a room. The horizontal strokes will express pink, the vertical blue: the scroll and flower are white; the lower part of the latter green.

In the 'Ant. d'Ercolano' is a picture, found at Pompeii, of the same subject, where Perseus holds up his chlamys, to conceal the head from Andromeda, who sees it reflected in a stream at her feet. But the learned academy, in their explanation, seem to have mistaken the intention of the painter.

FORUM.

Arrived at the Forum, or public square, it may be proper to take some slight notice of those points in the architecture of Pompeii, from which conclusion is drawn of its Greek origin. There may be little of its purity; but traces still remain sufficiently decisive to recall remembrances, although in many instances but faint, of the school from which they sprung.

If the whole of the plain below Pompeii be alluvial, which there is every reason to believe, the city must have originally been placed upon a promontory of lava, advancing into the sea.

Upon the edge or brow of this promontory we find one of those temples, surrounded by a portico of columns, of which neither the plan nor details are to be found in any instance of early Roman antiquity: both the one and the other being peculiar to Greece or her colonies.

The purest specimens of the Doric order vary, from the early columns of Corinth to the later of Athens, from four to six diameters in height: but these, it should be remarked, were used in public edifices, where grandeur of character and solidity of effect were required. The remains of the above-mentioned temple approach the earliest proportions. In some instances, this order at Pompeii is as slender as eight diameters, but the Greek character of the detail is always preserved, and it has no base. Barbarously executed, a curious method of ornamenting the capital will be observed to some of the columns of the Forum.

Whatever was the original form of the Ionic capital, it is certain that the most important specimens ever executed still remain upon the shores of Asia Minor, where the fronts and flanks are different in their form. At the temple of Apollo at Phygaleia, older than any of these, every face is made to correspond: a practice coinciding with most specimens of this order at Pompeii, and to which the Athenian architect was obliged to resort at each angle of his building.

The character of the Corinthian here accords precisely with that of the temple of Vesta at Tivoli; but this can hardly be called a Greek order, and its proportions seem to have been so far misunderstood at Pompeii, that its last ædile, accustomed to an eight diameter Doric, could allow a colonnade, in proportion less than six diameters, to be transformed into this order. The original more simple proportions of the Doric, loaded with a mass of incongruous plaster ornaments, of which every repetition differed in detail, was still further deprived of any approach to consistency, when delivered over to the painter to be finished with an endless variety of gaudy colours, covering every inch of its surface.

With the Greeks, architectural ornament may be compared with those parasitical plants, which, continually intertwining, climb to the tops of the loftiest trees, and pass from branch to branch, without injuring the individual grandeur of character in the various species they embellish. With this feeling, where profusion of decoration was introduced, in the more simple order, it was not carved, but the unbroken forms of the mouldings were preserved, and the detail was painted: whereas, with the Romans, all distinction of surface was frittered away in an endless maze of fret-work.

The repeated instances of the three orders, when found in a classic country, however, to the common eye, they may appear to resemble each other, are still worthy the attention of the architect or professional student, who may gather from them the history as well as refinement of their art; but from Pompeii little instruction of this kind can be drawn. It would be idle to give specimens of the detail, where columns are continually, by means of plaster, altered from one species to another; and of course those proportions of diameter to height, which the eye expects to vary with the several orders, everywhere violated.

The Forum was a space originally destined to negotiation,[1] either of merchants or others, whose arrangements or litigations took place in the open air. It was generally surrounded by a colonnade, over which was sometimes a second order with galleries, for the convenience of those who wished to view the shows; for it was the scene of the gladiatorial combats until the invention of the amphitheatre; when, by the removal of the games, the necessity for these galleries was obviated. Basilicæ were subsequently added, for the protection of the litigants and decision of causes, under shelter.

No city, however small, was without its Forum. It was the market-place for the sale of all sorts of goods, whether of rustics or citizens.[2] Under its porticoes were exercised various trades, liberal, servile, or sordid; and within them were arranged the taberna argentaria, thermopolia, and sometimes cloacina.

In the Forum was also the senate house; the curia, for the assemblies of augustals and priests, for cognizance of sacred matters; the comitia, for assemblies of the people; the nymphæum; ærarium, or treasury; record office, and public granaries.

The forum of Pompeii was thus surrounded by public and other buildings; but the particular destination of each must still remain in obscurity, since neither inscriptions nor other data remain, from which con-

---

[1] FESTUS.
[2] It was infested with barrow-women; thence called Foracia.

jecture can be fully borne out in assigning to each its ancient use. By the remains of the old arcade on the east side, it would appear, that at the period of the first eruption of Vesuvius, it was undergoing a total change in character, if not in form: the old arches were giving place to a colonnade of the Doric order, of which more than two of the three sides were already completed. The columns, 2 feet $3\frac{1}{2}$ inches in diameter, were of three sorts; of fine white caserta stone—of ancient yellowish tufa—and a third of brick, plastered.[1] They were 12 feet high.

Upon the epistylia over this colonnáde, at the south end, was an inscription, of which detached portions only remain; but the whole may be completed from another which appears to have been a duplicate found over a doorway in the street running from the Forum towards the Theatres.

EVMACHIA · L · F · SACERD · PVBLIC · NOMINE · SVO · ET ·
M · NVMISTRI · FRONTONIS · FILI · CHALCIDICVM ·
CRYPTAM · PORTICVM · CONCORDIAE · AVGVSTAE ·
PIETATI · SVA . PEQVNIA · FECIT · EADEMQVE ·
DEDICAVIT ·[2]

At the north end arose an edifice, which must have been more magnificent than any yet discovered in this

---

[1] It may be conjectured, that some of these originally belonged to a gallery above the arcade; which gallery might have been dispensed with on rebuilding after the earthquake. The columns were used for affixing tablets, with notices.—PROPERT., iii, 23.

[2] The three last lines are only two in the original marble, and are consequently in smaller capitals than the first.

city. Its flight of steps, the solid-looking podium and platform, flanking triumphal arches, and spacious portico of Corinthian columns, nearly as large as those of our cathedral church of St. Paul,[1] as well as its singular interior, all bespeak a building of importance; and conjecture, without the least foundation, has attributed it to the worship of the king of gods. The interior was ornamented with a row of eight columns, of the Ionic order, on each side, 1 foot $10\frac{1}{2}$ inches in diameter; 3 feet 8 inches asunder, and about the same distance from the wall. There was, possibly, another order above, to support the beams of the ceiling. The walls were painted in compartments of dark colours below, with red and black above. The floor was paved with marble, in lozenge-shaped pieces within a border of mosaic. Upon this latter were found the trunk of a colossal statue, twice the size of life, two feet upon the same scale, with very complicated sandals, and a large face, all of marble.

At the further end were three low, vaulted cells,[2] no higher than the internal order; and behind them ran a passage, with a stair-case, probably to a gallery supported by these columns. The clear space in the inside was about 42 feet by 28 feet 6 inches.

The decurions were so by birth or election, which could be extended to strangers; since we find individuals of this degree in more than one town;[3] not forfeiting it

---

[1] 3 feet 8 inches diameter; probably approaching 40 feet in height.

[2] It may be observed, that a similar space, upon a smaller scale, is divided off in the temple of Isis, in another part of this city.

[3] By a law of Pompey, renewed by Trajan.—PLINY, x, 95-96.

by domiciliation or incolition, but holding the same rank in both the one and the other curia.

That the deliberations might be more solemn, the senate house in Rome could only be a temple, or consecrated place;[1] while each senator, before taking his seat, made an offering upon the altar of the god.[2] And as the decurions of the coloniæ, or municipia, held the same privileges in their respective corporations which the senators exercised at Rome, their deliberations may have been carried on with similar solemnities, and their place of meeting in like manner have been sanctified. Admitting this to be probable, the edifice before us may be conjectured to have been the Senaculum; and if so, the cells were, in all probability, depositories for records; and the platform in front, the pulpitum, whence the people were addressed.[3]

The three columns in the Roman Forum, hitherto called of Jupiter Stator, have been found to belong to a building very similar in plan to this, but with its portico much more lengthened. The Roman antiquaries consider it to have been the Comitium.

---

[1] GELL., xiv, 7. VIRGIL, Æneid, vii, 174, identifies the great temple of Laurentum with the curia:

"Hoc illis curia templum."

In the lines following will be seen the manner in which such places were decorated.

[2] CICERO, Dom.

[3] Looking towards this building, on the ground to the right of this platform, a sun-dial has been found, similar in principle to that in the Elgin collection.

PLATE XLIV.

1. Supposed Senaculum, called upon the spot the temple of Jupiter. But whether this edifice was really dedicated to that god must at least remain doubtful, until some authority presents itself. Under the steps were three arched vaults.
2. Triumphal arch. This seems to have been a recent building: it was of bricks and rubble, fronted with slabs and ornaments of white marble and stucco. It was imagined in the first edition of this work, that the intention had been to erect another corresponding with this on the other side of the steps of the temple; but the more recent excavations have rendered this conjecture at least doubtful.
3. This building was probably the place of meeting of some associated members of the government; perhaps the augustals, who had cognizance of sacred matters. It was spacious; 83 feet from front to rear, by 60 wide, and paved in compartments with large slabs of variegated marble, with red spots. In front was a portico of eight columns of fine white caserta stone or marble. Around the interior were niches, and in the centre a pedestal or altar. Opposite the entrance was a wide recess over a podium.
4. Temple, within an enclosure, 57 feet 6 inches by 50 feet 7 inches. In front was the altar remaining very perfect. (See Plate LXIII.)

    The temple was small; its external dimensions 15 feet 6 inches by 13 feet 8 inches. It was placed upon a raised basement, the steps to ascend which were from the rear on each side.
5. On one side of this entrance was a staircase, under

which were holes, with amphoræ.[1] On the other a passage through several divisions conducted to a subterranean apartment, as well as to the rear of the foregoing temple.

On three sides of the area to which this opened, was a cryto portico, with windows into an open colonnade which ranged before it, and immediately opposite the entrance was a large semi-circular recess. Behind this recess, in a niche within the cryto portico, was found a statue[2] of a female, of indifferent workmanship, upon a pedestal, bearing the following inscription:

EVMACHIAE · L · F
SACERD · PVBL
FVLLONES

This area was 158 feet by 92 feet 4 inches, including the open portico.

The cryto portico communicated by a flight of steps down to the adjoining street which leads from the Theatres. Over the opening at the foot of these steps is the inscription, given at page 147, by which we are informed, that this same lady, at her own expense, and in the name of herself and son, raised and dedicated the Chalcidicum and cryto portico. The latter was doubtless the building in question, to which we should also be inclined to refer the former of these names, had not the above-mentioned inscription, in enabling us to restore another upon the epistylia of the colonnade at the south end of the Forum, rendered it doubtful

[1] "Nulla est in angiporto amphora quam non impleant quippe qui vesicam plenam vini habeant."—MAC., Sat. II, 12.

[2] This statue, immediately upon its discovery, was pulled down, to be transferred to the Royal Museum, and the pedestal taken in pieces, to be deposited with other fragments in the space before the temple (4), now used as a magazine for such remains; but a subsequent order from Naples has replaced the statue upon its re-erected pedestal.

whether the Chalcidicum were not in its more immediate vicinity.

The street which runs along the side of this building conducts, though not in a direct line, to the theatres: it is now cleared, and contains two fountains, one opposite the foot of the steps up to the crypto porticus. The footway on the south side is of cement, studded with fragments of coloured stones. The whole street is regularly built with pilasters in front of the houses. Upon the wall forming the angle between this street and an alley running nearly at right angles with it to the Scava della Regina Carolina, are painted twelve gods and goddesses, over a little altar. (Shown Plate LXXVII.) Carriages were prevented by a step from entering the Forum from this quarter.

On many of the houses are the owners' names. One is of Vettius. (See page 116, second Inscrip.)

6. Old arcade; which was about to be replaced by the Doric portico.

7. This space next the wall was probably left uncovered, for the admission of light.

Another street here runs in a different direction, southward, towards the theatre. In it lived a Terence; also Sabinus and Rufus. (See page 116.)

8, 9, 10. Of these three large apartments, if they were not Chalcidica it would be difficult to guess the destination. Vitruvius speaks of the treasury and prison as contiguous to the Forum. The former were not only for the lodgement of money, but any thing which could be considered the riches of the state, as records of laws.[1]

11. A Janus. Suetonius classes the triumphal arches with these buildings, multiplied by Domitian through Rome. A quadriga, or some sort of triumphal statue, of metal, seems usually to have crowned the summit; while their

---

[1] The Chalcidica of the Basilica of Æmilia had a semicircular end, with recesses for the judges' seats.—See Nibby's 'Nardini.'

arched roof formed frequently a protecting canopy to imperial vanity, exhibited in more perishable materials. The statue of Pompey, at the base of which Cæsar expired, was by order of Augustus removed out of the curia, and placed under a marble Janus, over against the theatre called by his name. When sufficiently large, they afforded cover to the merchants from sun or rain. This was perhaps their original intention, and the mode of their decoration and after practice.[1]

12. Pedestals for groups or equestrian statues.
13. Pedestals for statues.
14. Staircases to the galleries, and second story of the basilica.

The Basilica was connected with the portico of the Forum by an uncovered court. In the sides of the piers between the two latter, are grooves for the insertion of wood or iron work, from which we may conclude that there were doors, or a railing of separation, between them. Steps from this court led up to the basilica, through the three central intercolumniations, and two door-ways, opening under the galleries.

The Basilicæ were peculiarly constructed, to receive crowds of people. They were, according to Victor, courts for the administration of justice, and exchanges for the assembly of merchants in rainy or doubtful weather. It should be, says Vitruvius, on the least exposed side of the Forum, with chalcidica at the end; where was also the tribunal. Six columns, elevated upon a podium, at Pompeii, enclosed the place of the Duumvir for justice, with his council, assessores, apparitores, lictors, and scribes; whence, from the curule chair, and distinguished by the insignia of the sword and spear, set upright before him, he delivered his dicta, after swearing upon the altar in front to decide according to law and his judgment.[2]

---

[1] SUETONIUS, in Aug., 31; CICERO, Phil., 6, 5.
[2] CIC., Acad. Q., 47.

The construction of the basilica is worthy of observation, inasmuch as it is said to have formed the prototype of the original church for Christian worship.[1] At Pompeii the principal roof, called the testudo, was upheld by twenty-eight columns, of the Ionic order, 3 feet 7 inches diameter.[2] It rose above the rest of the building, and each end was finished with a pediment. This was surrounded at some distance by a wall; between which and the columns on each side was a low portico, and above the latter a gallery for the convenience of spectators.

The roof over the gallery was formed to fall all round, from the wall towards the centre; its eaves being probably kept considerably below the architrave of the principal structure, for the admission of light between the capitals of the columns.[3]

The walls of the basilica are daubed with imitations of red, green, and yellow marbles, in large blocks; smaller semi-columns, of the Corinthian order and similar in dimensions with the four at the entrance, at intervals supported the ends of the beams of the gallery above.

[1] Whittingham imagines these buildings to have been open at the sides. A temple of Venus at Aphrodisias, converted to a church in the age of Constantine, shows this not to have been the case.

[2] Upon this wall are scratched many inscriptions. Amongst them is "C. Pumidius Dipilus heic fuit ad nonas Octobreis M. Lepid. Q. Catul. Cos." These were consuls 77 A.C., the year Sylla died. In another part is the word BASSILICA.

[3] The account Vitruvius gives of the basilica to which he was architect, varies essentially from the rules he lays down for those usual in Italy; which were constructed of two orders of columns, with a pluteum between, and the floor of the gallery laid upon the lower pillars. But in that built by himself, one order reached from the floor to the testudo, or roof, and accessory pilasters were introduced for the support of the gallery. The great size of the columns in the Pompeian basilica, compared with the smaller against the wall, seems to point it out as built upon the approved plan of Vitruvius; and thus the text, with submission, presumes.

The floor of the porticoes appears to have been of cement: under the centre part earth only remains, with a channel against the columns, and holes at intervals, for the water to sink into wells, or cisterns, formed beneath for its reception. .

16. Cistern, to receive the water from the channels into which it fell from the roof.
17. Tribunal. This was raised, and had a cella, or space, underneath.
18. Pedestal, which sustained a statue of bronze, of which the legs only were found.
19. Chalcidica? this part might have been open.
20. Sinkings, to receive the water which fell from the roof, and through these ran into the cisterns.
21. Side entrances from the adjoining streets.
22. Entrance to the enclosure of a temple. It may also be approached from the Forum by other openings. No name has hitherto, with sufficient authority, been applied to this edifice. On the spot, a portion of a female statue, found therein, has induced the excavators to assign it to Venus; while the pictures found within its enclosure do not afford much better ground for supposing it of any other divinity. Around the walls of the porticoes, at two feet six inches from the ground, runs a series of paintings, of dwarfs and architectural subjects. In one corner is a painting of Achilles and Agamemnon; in another Hector tied to the car of Achilles; and in an apartment is a picture of Bacchus and Silenus. Pygmies are from the Nile; and the latter picture may have had reference to the god here worshipped, with whose rites some mixture of other ceremonies may have been celebrated. This temple was erected at a period when the taste of Rome, tired of making useless prayers to the old divinities, had brought from Greece and Egypt mystery and superstition. The religion of Isis, Bacchus, Ceres, veiled in obscurity, had once become the cloak for the most

degrading debauchery and inhuman orgies; but the attempt at extermination only served to incite the curiosity, and superinduce the renewal of rites so peculiarly congenial to the feelings of this people. On the accession of Augustus, the zeal of fanaticism prevailed; and the temples, destroyed by the policy of the old government, were rebuilt, with additional splendour, under subsequent emperors. Otho patronised, and Vespasian, in gratitude, favoured Serapis;[1] the propitiation of whom was believed to have obtained him not only the government, but an imaginary power of working miracles.[2]

The area is surrounded by a portico, 12 feet 2 inches wide, covered with beams of timber. It consisted of 48 stone columns, originally of the Doric order, $5\frac{1}{2}$ diameters high; but subsequently transformed, by means of plaster, into Corinthian; the capital borrowing a part of the shaft, already too short. They are nearly all different, both in form and colours. The architraves are a horizontal arch, two pieces to each column; the metopes and mutules are filled up with tiles and stucco; the whole painted in an endless variety of ornaments.[3]

The lower third of the columns is reeded, and painted yellow; the upper part, fluted, is white. At their bases runs a channel, to convey away the water which fell from the eaves; and before each was a terminal statue; one remains perfect, but not of very fine workmanship.[4]

---

[1] Ammianus describes the atrium of the Serapion as surrounded with columns and paintings, "ut nihil ambitiosius."

[2] Dio—Suetonius—Tacitus. He restored sight by spitting in the eyes. Capt. Light mentions a curious modern instance of this superstition. —See his 'Journal.'

[3] These columns are 2 feet 4 inches in diameter, 13 feet high, and have 20 flutes. The intercolumniation is 7 feet 2 inches. The entablature in height 3 feet 4 inches; of which the architrave is only 6 inches.

[4] See Plate LIV.

Here was also found a consular figure, of better style, in white marble; and a statue of a female called a Venus. In front of the steps to the temple is the great altar; on the top of this a piece of black stone has three places for fire, the ashes of the victims remaining. On its west and east sides are duplicate inscriptions, recording that the quartumviri named, placed it at their own expense:

M PORCIVS·M·F·L SEXTILIVS·L·F·CN CORNELIVS·CN·F· A CORNELIVS·A·F·IIIIVIR·D·P·S·F·LOCAR·

Ascended by sixteen steps the temple itself is placed upon an elevated basement, which is now stripped of its exterior; and if the building was ever surrounded by columns, they no longer exist. At the angles are pilasters, two feet diameter. The water was spouted from the roof by large projecting lions' heads.

23. Cell of the temple, with the pedestal for the statue in the interior.
24. Altar, in front of the steps, inscribed as above.
There is another pedestal or altar, marked also 24.
25. Pedestals.
26. Room, in which was found the picture of Bacchus and Silenus.[1] This fresco had been anciently removed from another situation to that it now occupies, and is fastened very neatly with iron cramps and cement, so as to require some examination to discover the fact.[2]
27. Magazines, 110 feet long, containing architectural fragments. They were possibly horrea, or public granaries; as in a recess (at 28,) are the public corn measures, similar to those near the Agora at Athens. They are cylindrical perforations: the bottom was false, and when removed allowed the measured corn to run out.

[1] Vignette, page 165.
[2] At Stabia, pictures separated from and leaning against the wall have been found.

At Rome the poor received a monthly quantum of grain; at first at a low expense, but subsequently, by the law of Clodius, gratis.[1]

29. Door-way, and
30. Arch-way into the back street; which is 19 feet wide.
31. Fountains.
32. Shops. Between two of these and the magazine (27) were prisons, secured by gratings of iron.
33. Old Triumphal Arch, the angle of which is built into that of the temple. The opening is 12 feet 9 inches wide. On each side are two columns with a niche. One of the latter contains a fountain.
34. Opening from the street to a Portico, beneath which are arranged 8 recesses or shops. The first contains a circular short pillar or trapezophoron, perhaps to support a table. The fifth has a pedestal under a niche with doors on each side communicating with the rear. The last, small in its dimensions, contains also a pedestal. In the angle beyond was a staircase. A series of pedestals are also ranged against the walls in front of these shops. This Portico appears to have had two orders of columns, Ionic and Corinthian.
35. Entrance to one of two houses excavated by the General Championet, and commonly known by his name. In one were found four skeletons of women, denoted by their trinkets, bracelets, earrings, and money; some little of gold and silver, but principally of brass. The antiquities found in this excavation were taken to Paris.
36. Tetrastyle cavædium, represented Plate xxxix.
37. Tablinum.
38. Peristyle.
39. Side entrance.
40. Entrance to the adjoining house.
41. Cavædium.
42. Tablinum.

[1] Livy.

POMPEII.

VIEW OF THE FORUM & BASILICA.

43. Peristyle.
44. Triclinium.
45, 46. The ground hence slopes abruptly, and the houses in this part are in a very ruined state; but they had a fine view towards the bay.

On five pieces of frieze, in the Forum, are the fragments of an inscription, alluded to, page 147.

L · F · SACERD · PVB—O · ET · M · NVMISTRI · FRONT—
HALCI—DICVM · CRYPT—CORDIAE · AVGVSTA—
VNIA · FEC—DEMQVE · DEDICAVIT ·

47. Apartment behind the Temple, marked 4.
48. Large Apartment or Magazine, 72 feet by 55 feet 4 inches.

PLATE XLV.

General view of the Forum and Basilica, as they existed 1818, from the spot in the plan marked A. Reference to the foregoing plan will afford the best explanation to this plate.

In the distance is Mount Lactarius, ending in the promontory of Surrentum.

PLATE XLVI.

View of the south end of the Forum and the basilica. The three entrances to the apartments 8, 9, 10 on the plan, are seen to the left; beyond these the door to the street of the houses of General Championet. On the right is the Janus and pedestals. The remains of the basilica are seen in the centre. At the farther end of it is the elevated tribunal; in the front of which is the pedestal (18).

PLATE XLVII.

View of the Forum from the point C. Some idea may here be obtained of the ornamented capitals, mentioned page 144; but they are very ill executed. Beyond the Janus is a piece of brickwork, with flat arches to receive stucco-work. It is the beginning of the street leading to the theatre, and part of the wall of the crypto portico surrounding a space excavated since this view was made.

PLATE XLVIII.

View of the Forum, from the interior of the cell of the Senaculum.
The distant mountain is Lactarius. The small columns on the right are supposed to have supported a gallery, mentioned at page 148.

Engraved by Chas Heath.

POMPEII.

VIEW OF THE FORUM AND BASILICA.

PLATE 47.

Engraved by C.Heath

POMPEII.
VIEW IN THE FORUM.

POMPEII.

VIEW OF THE FORUM FROM THE TEMPLE OF JUPITER.

PLATE 49

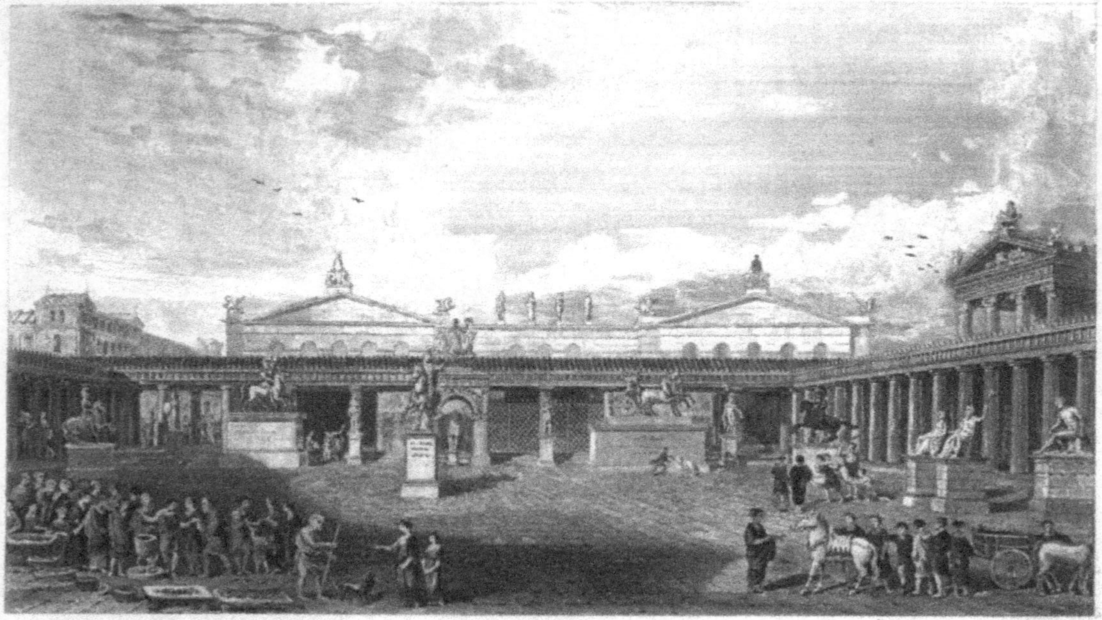

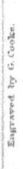

Engraved by G. Cooke.

POMPEII.

POMPEII.

ORNAMENTS FROM THE BASILICA.

PLATE XLIX.

Restored view of the Forum. This view is given that some idea may be obtained of the general appearance of the several buildings at the south end, where was the inscription, page 159. The surrounding portico, or colonnade, of the Doric order, will be observed; over the end of which appear the three buildings marked on the plan 8, 9, 10. The Janus in the centre, and pedestals, are the precise forms and proportions of those which remain, as will be seen by a reference to the view showing their actual state: whatever they sustained no longer exists, or has been removed. The tetrastyle, Ionic front, and pediment of the basilica, appear to the right.

The figures inserted in this plate are all taken from paintings found in the city, and principally from one representing its Forum. But we needed not this picture to know that Forums were adorned with statues of every description.

PLATE L.

This plate contains a plan of one of the columns of the basilica. They are formed of tiles, or thin bricks, presenting their angles in the alternate courses, so as to form a ground for the plaster fillets, and flutes. The plaster is peculiarly good, and has almost the hardness of porcelain.

Also two Antefixes, from the basilica. One is ornamented with a head *persona*, the other, 14 inches high, with foliage, of which the lower part was painted green, the upper yellow. Two forms of tiles were used in ancient buildings: the imbrex, placed in regular rows, to receive the shower; and the tegula,[1] which covered and prevented the rain from penetrating the joints. The latter were finished at the eaves with upright ornaments, shaped as those before us; and which were repeated also at the junction of these tiles, along the ridge.

These ornaments are called by Pliny personæ.[2] He refers their invention to Dibutades, a Sicyonian potter, established at Corinth, who called them *protypes*,[3] being stamped in front only: those upon the ridge were an after-thought of the same artist, and, worked on all sides, were named *ectypes*. From the circumstance of their having been originally formed of a plastic material, the ornamented ridges still continued to be called *plastes*, after Byzes of Naxos had introduced marble in their execution,[4] of which material he cut all these ornaments, as well as the whole covering of the roof; but still adhering to the original form and detail. His contemporaries decreed an inscription to his memory, whereby the honour of so ingenious an invention might be secured to him.[5]

The tiles at the temple at Ecbatana were of silver.

[1] Isidor.—In Livy, 26, 23, the victory upon the apex of a pediment, struck by lightning, is arrested in its fall, and hangs upon the antefixes. See also the speech of Cato, in 34, 4.

[2] "Cretea persona."—Lucretius, 4, 498. They were probably at first masks: "Personæ pallentis hiatum."—Juvenal, 3, 175.

[3] Pliny, 35.

[4] For the only published specimen, see the 'Antiquities of Attica.'

[5] The γραπτοι τυποι, in the very corrupted fragment of the Υψιπυλη of Euripides, preserved in Galen, were, in all probability, the painted antefixes.

POMPEIANA. 163

Alexander pillaged them; but Antiochus found some still remaining.[1]

In the lower part of the plate is a terra cotta eaves tiles, in which the simple drawing of Athens, more florid in Ionian specimens, is carried a step further; though complicated, it is distinct from the confusion of the Roman.

[1] POLYBIUS, 10, 24.

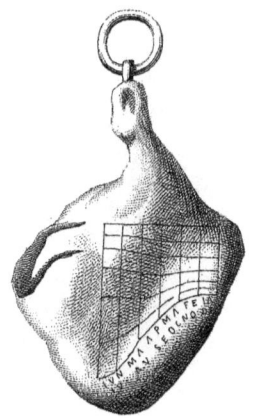

TEMPLES.

An essential feature in the temples of Pompeii, as distinguished from those of Greece, is to be observed in the podium or basement, upon which they were elevated. In the religious edifices of an early age, no such character appears: they were placed upon two or three steps only, if steps they should be termed, when evidently not proportioned for convenience of access to the interior, but calculated rather with a view to the general effect of the whole structure.

In the temples of Greece, we view architecture in its purest and most simple form: in the age of Titus we see that it had already reached the last period of complication and decline. To trace the connecting links is not the intention of this work, though perhaps, or rather certainly, the same causes operated throughout the chain; namely, the progress of society, and the changes of religion. The founders of cities invariably chose the highest ground for the Hiera of the deity;[1] while, in the crowded lanes of the lower town, artificial means were requisite, to give to the temples of the imported gods that dignity which the Athenian, Eleusinian, and Delphic structures acquired from their natural sites.

[1] VIRGIL, Æn., 5, 759; and 7, 171.

POMPEII.

VIEW OF THE TEMPLE, AT THE NORTH END OF THE FORUM.

PLATE 57.

Engraved by J. Le Keux.

POMPEII.

PLATE LI.

View of the Senaculum, or temple of Jupiter. To the left are the remains of a triumphal arch; and perhaps another, correspondent, was to have been built on the other side of the steps of the temple. These steps, flanked by pedestals, are singular in their plan. A platform, or terrace, is formed, dividing them into two flights, and extending to the front, where was probably a rail, whence the orator spoke. From Cicero we learn, that Licinius Crassus introduced the custom of turning the face to the Forum, and not to the senate, when he addressed the people.

This edifice, to whatever purpose it may have been appropriated, is described page 148. Behind the farthest flanking pedestal is a door of entrance to the arched vaults, formed under the steps.

PLATE LII.

Restored view of the foregoing temple and north end of the Forum. On the left is the Doric colonnade, great part of which remained to be completed; over it rises the great granary or horrea. On the right is the building marked 3 upon the plan, and referred to page 150.

168   POMPEIANA.

This temple brings to our recollection a passage of Gibbon; who remarks, that "In the commonwealth of Athens and Rome, the modest simplicity of private houses announced the equal condition of freedom; whilst the sovereignty of the people was represented by the majestic edifices destined to public use." The part to the right had perhaps a second order, as two sizes of columns are found upon the spot; but this restoration was imagined before the excavation had fully laid open the part beyond the building marked 3.

PLATE LIII.

View of the temple of Venus or Bacchus.

The plan of the Forum (Plate XLIV) may be referred to in explanation of this plate. The steps of the temple have been much dislocated, and the altar thrown out of the level, by the earthquake, which preceded the destruction of the city. The columns of the peribolus, originally Doric, have been altered to Corinthian. The remains of the Senaculum are seen over the wall which separates this enclosure from the Forum.

POMPEII.

VIEW OF THE TEMPLE OF BACCHUS.

POMPEII.

Engraved by Chs. Heath.

PLATE 55.

PLATE 56.

Engraved by H.Moses.

POMPEII.

PAINTINGS.

PLATE LIV.

View of the temple of Venus or Bacchus, with Mount
Vesuvius in the distance. A terminal statue is here
shown. One appears to have been before each column.
The channel to receive and convey away the water
which fell into it from the eaves of the roof of the
portico, will be observed. Upon the altar was an
inscription, repeated on two sides (see page 157). The
piece of sculpture is a fragment of the frieze.

PLATES LV, LVI.

Around the walls of the peribolus of the temple of Bacchus
are introduced divers representations of architectural
subjects and pygmies; whence it obtained the name of
the House of the Dwarfs, until the year 1817, when
an entire excavation having been effected in that
quarter, it was found to contain a temple.

The painter in these subjects has given to the proportions
of children, heads bearing the character of grown men,
leaving the extremities always unfinished. Some of
these are given in the Plates LV to LXII, more with a
view to the architecture they represent, than as works
of art. The buildings in the back-ground are always

a faint blue or white, and the trees badly daubed. The figures of a dark blackish red, generally less well preserved, are difficult to make out.

SENECA moralises upon the unnatural custom of planting gardens upon the house tops, which enhanced considerably their value. It is not uncommon in Italy and Malta to the present day.

The ornament separating these two subjects is a threshold, in mosaic.

PLATES LVII, LVIII.

These paintings are highly curious, as exhibiting some resemblance of houses, perhaps in situations removed from the immediate protection of a town, or where it might be considered expedient in their construction to afford the means of defence. Each is separate, and provided with a tower.

How necessary such appendages were, may be concluded from accounts left us of the predatory nature of ancient warfare. In modern Greece these buildings still retain their ancient use, as well as designation, πυργος. Galen tells us, the pyrgos and tyrsis were synonymous: that they were common may be gathered from the passage of Hippocrates, which calls forth the remark. Upon the top was the heliasterion, warm in winter, cool in summer. One of these has a shed, to intercept the rays of the sun by day, or dew of the night; another has a strong resemblance to the *motivo* of the roof of the choragic monument of Lysicrates at Athens; a third has a vertical piece through the apex of the pediment, the germ of the Gothic pinnacle.

Engraved by Chas. Heath.

POMPEII.

PAINTINGS IN THE TEMPLE OF BACCHUS

POMPEII.

PAINTINGS AT THE TEMPLE OF BACCHUS.

POMPEII.

PAINTINGS AT THE TEMPLE OF BACCHUS.

PLATE LIX.

The advancing colonnade, without a roof, strikes at first as being useless; but it was probably intended for training vines, of which the interclustered leaves and fruit formed a much cooler and more agreeable shade than stone.

In the distance appears a marine villa.

PLATE LX.

Many authors of antiquity mention the pygmies,[1] three spans long; they were famous for continually warring against the cranes; but here is one sustaining a much more unequal combat, which he appears to have escaped from, only by means of the less fortunate fate of his companion.[2]

The temple is singular, from having a curved pediment. It is guarded in the Egyptian manner, by sphinges. In the front is an altar, with Mercury, and two other pygmy figures.

[1] Homer—Aristotle—Pliny.
[2] There is a subject which might class with these amongst the terra cottas of the British Museum, No. 36.

PLATE LXI

Is a curious architectural subject. Pliny, describing his villa, says the hippodrome had cypresses planted around. A sort of figure appears running down to a boat: the perspective of these latter does not seem well understood.
The painting is obliterated to the right.

PLATE LXII.

An architectural subject, with a pyrgos.

PLATE LXIII.

View of a temple, discovered 1817. It is placed within an enclosure, about 57 feet 6 inches by 50 feet 7 inches; the wall of which is formed in brickwork, to receive a stucco exterior. Steps,[1] at the rear, led up to the adytum, or cell, placed upon a podium, 9 feet high; and within is the pedestal for the statue. The altar, the only part perfect, is of white marble, the whole

[1] See Plan of Forum, Plate XLIV, 4.

POMPEII.

PAINTINGS.

POMPEII.

PAINTINGS.

POMPEII.

VIEW OF THE NEW TEMPLE WEST SIDE OF THE FORUM.

about 4 feet 6 inches high; some have imagined the sculpture upon it to represent Cicero sacrificing, from a supposed resemblance in the principal figure to that great orator. The victim is led by the popa, naked to the waist, with his malleus and tucked-up clothes. The sacrificator is a magistrate or augustal, with his lictors and fasces; a boy follows, with the simpulum, patera, and sacred vitta. In the back-ground is the temple, decorated with garlands. On the east, or opposite side, is an oak wreath, with olives; on the north, under a festoon, some implements of sacrifice; and on the south a suspended vitta and lituus.

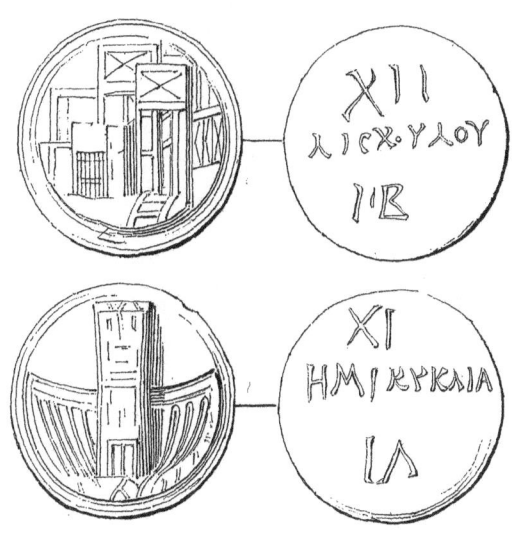

THEATRES.

The theatres of Rome, for a long time of wood, were commonly open at top; and the scenic representations took place in open day. The seats were occupied at random by the first comers,[1] until the time of Scipio Africanus:[2] but by the Roscian Law the lower fourteen were reserved for the dignified orders. Under Pompey they first became regular structures; and subsequently

---

[1] *Vide* ULPIAN, in Demosth. Olint.

[2] He separated the senators from the people; but, at the Circus, the former had no privilege until the reign of Claudius.

Augustus[1] undertook to regulate the disorder which continually arose amongst the spectators in a space so undefined, and of which every part was easily accessible to any individual who had once made good an entry.[2]

When Augustus assigned to each order its place, he distributed the military distinct from the populace. Separate cunei and cinctions were allotted to the priests, the vestals, and various distinguished orders. To the senators were reserved the seats in the immediate vicinity of the orchestra, and amongst them sat the ambassadors of foreign nations;[3] while women and strangers were withdrawn to the galleries, which ranged around the upper part of the cavea. Julius Cæsar had before extended to children and grand-children the privileges of their fathers.

Three great divisions are distinguishable in the theatre at Pompeii. In the lowest near the orchestra, the seats or steps of greater width, mark the place whence the civil magistrates, the college of priests, and those distinguished by the offices they held, or the honours they had received, saw the performances, placed in their curule chairs, and bisellii or privileged seats. The middle seats, less ample in their dimensions, had cushions; while the gallery above, considered effeminate, was covered over.

---

[1] Suetonius, in Aug., 44.
[2] Tacitus, 13, 54.
[3] For the observances imposed, see the Prologue to the 'Pænulus' of Plautus.

"Venimus ad sedes, ubi pullâ sordida veste
Inter femineas spectabat turba cathedras :
Nam quæcunque pateat sub aperto libera cœlo,
Aut eques, aut nivei loca densavêre tribuni."[1]

The stage, or proscenium, was considerably elevated, and the scene was richly decorated with ornaments of architecture and paintings. Behind this was the post-scenium, for the actors to retire into. Near the theatre was usually a portico, to which the audience withdrew in the event of unfavorable weather.

[1] Titus Calphurnius, Eclog. 7. But this was the age of Diocletianus.

PLATE LXIV.

Plan of the Quarter of the Theatres.

Two adjoining theatres existed at Pompeii: one, considerably smaller than the other, was covered. Advantage seems to have been taken, in placing them, of a hollow in the side of the hill. They were approached from the Forum by an octastyle Ionic loggia, or propylea, opening by two door-ways into a portico of the Doric order,[1] adjoining an ample area, in the midst of which stood the Greek temple.[2]

In this portico were found some articles of gold and silver, and an emerald ring, probably dropped by their possessor in his haste to escape.

1. A fountain.
2. A marble patera, or tazza.
3. Pedestal, inscribed

M · CLAVDIO · M · F · MARCELLO · PATRONO

The Greek temple was placed on a spot rather elevated, and considerably so with respect to the theatres and great square. Little more than the foundations now exist; for it seems to have been despoiled even before the destruction of the city. The columns, of which some of the lower frusta remain, are 3 feet 10 inches in diameter, diminishing to 3 feet. The abacus is 4 feet 11 inches square, and the whole capital peculiar, inasmuch as the stone out of which it is worked

---

[1] Columns, 1 foot 9 inches in diameter, 13 feet 4 inches high, upon two steps. In the lower step was a water channel.

[2] Between the columns were iron bars, to confine the crowd to the porticus.

includes no part of the shaft; while its great depth, 1 foot 10¼ inches, as well as bold projection, denote a very ancient character. In the best examples of the Doric order, there is a beautiful continuity of the column into its capital, not adhered to in this. The intercolumniation is one diameter and two ninths; but the whole temple is so dilapidated, that it is no longer possible to ascertain how many columns either the front or flanks presented.[1]

4. Pen for victims.
5. Altars.
6. This has been called a bidental. Places struck by lightning were regarded with singular horror, as devoted to the wrath of heaven. The spot was enclosed and an altar raised, whereon bidentes were in expiation sacrificed. Eight Doric tufa columns, 1 foot 4 inches in diameter, here upheld a circular epistylium, whereon was an Oscan inscription, stating that Nitrebius, thrice high priest, or magistrate, placed it.

NITREBIIS · TR · MED · TVF
ΑΑΜΑΝΑΦΦΕD

It was, however, more probably, the covering of a well, necessary to the ceremonies at the temple; and what has been called an altar, perforated, was a puteal. The objection urged to this is, that it has a rough inside, and had no rope marks. The former, puteals very often were: it is 3 feet 7 inches in diameter: the whole building 12 feet 5 inches. The aamanaphphed, to favour the former supposition, has been translated "amphi sepsit," and "septo conclusit;" but the same word occurs over the Nolan gate (see page 97), which can hardly have been enclosed.

The term puteal has been preferred, because there does not

---

[1] See Plate LXVII.

appear sufficient authority for concluding that a well-cover was placed over all places struck by lightning. According to Festus, Scribonius Libo removed one into such a situation; but it would be difficult to show that the structure alluded to by him was not the same as the depository of the razor and severed whetstone of Actius Nævius, which Cicero treats as one of those antiquities of the capital too remote in their origin for the truth of history.[1]

A restoration is given as the vignette to the preface: where all above the cornice is imaginary, but the form of the top shows it to have had a covering. The inscription is also there given.[2]

7. A semicircular seat, or hemicyclon.
8. Entrance to the cunei of the great theatre, and
9. A second entrance from another street. These conducted into a corridor, or arched passage of communication under the gallery, from which six doors opened

---

[1] 1 'De Div.,' 17.

[2] In the early excavations of Herculaneum was found another Oscan inscription. An oblong table, supported by three animal legs, was inscribed upon the top:

HERENTATEISSVM

And round the edge:

L · SLABIIS · L · AVKIL · MEDDIX · TVFTIKS
HERENTATEN ::: RVKINAI ' PRVΦΦED

The foregoing has been often published, but a wide lacunar always left in the latter part, through which a different reading of the whole has crept with every repetition.—See Passeri—Walchius—Remondini—Ignarra—Lanzi—Rosini—Hayter—Sir W. Drummond.

opposite as many flights of steps, separating the cinctions into cunei.
10. Staircase to the upper gallery.
11. This flight of steps descended to the square, vulgarly called the Soldiers' Quarters; or, by turning to the left, into the open area between that square and the theatre.[1] Hence it communicated with the privileged seats, through 12 down to 13, as well as with the stage and postscenium, or room for the actors.
14. The stage, or pulpitum, upon which the actors performed. Constructed of wood, this part of a theatre can never remain perfect. Underneath is a hollow space, with foundation walls, bounded by the dotted line;[2] and marks show the floor beams to have been eighteen inches asunder.

In front of this, seven recesses probably mark the place of the musicians, called Thymelici, because they stood in the orchestra, upon a pulpitum, named Thymele.[3] The centre is semicircular, and the middle of the three on each side contains steps. At the back of the wall in which they are formed, are nine chasings, or grooves, as if to fix and keep steady some wood-work. A space between this and the front of the stage is much deeper than any other part, and contains eight square stones, with sunk holes, which seem to have been for fixing

---

[1] Perhaps in this area the actors underwent the punishment they sometimes met with, at the caprice of the audience. Lucian tells us that they were on some occasions whipped.

[2] Vitruvius gives a long account of the vases placed in ancient theatres for the purpose of promoting the passage of sound. None of these have been found in the theatre of Pompeii; and himself states that they were not much known even in Rome. The whole looks like a theoretical refinement; though a recent traveller seems to have found them in a Syrian theatre.

[3] 'Isidor.,' 18, 19. The whole of this may serve to illustrate 'Pollux,' in 4, 19.

posts, or some part of the moveable machinery.[1] The aulæum might have been at this place. Apuleius distinguishes between it and the siparium: "Aulæo subducto et complicitis sipariis." The former was, probably, the drop scene: the latter merely drawn before the doors, and by means of it the stage might have been contracted.

It is almost as difficult to conjecture, as it is impossible to ascertain, the finishing of the front of the scene, so few data remain for fancy to enlarge upon.

There were three doorways, through which the actors appeared upon the stage.

In the theatre were found,

M · M · HOLCONI · RVFVS · ET CELER
CRYPTAM · TRIBVNAL THEATRVM · S · P ·
AD · DECVS · COLONIÆ

and

M · HOLCONIO · M · F · RVFO · IIVIR · I · D
QVINQVIENS · ITER · QVINQ · TRIB · MILAR
FLAMINI · AVG · PATR · COLON · D · D ·

From the word colonia has been inferred, that Pompeii had ceased being a municipium before its final destruction. Publius Sylla, nephew of the dictator, led a colony into the Pompeian territory. Under Julius and Augustus, others followed: but the city appears, in the time of Cicero, notwithstanding, to have retained its privileges as a municipium; and it is so called by Statius.

From another street, the lower part of the theatre might be approached through an Ionic[2] loggia (15), portico (16),

---

[1] It may be remarked, that a great deal of wood-work and framing was found over the stage at Herculaneum, evidently for the purpose of managing machinery, as well as covering it over.

[2] This Ionic has no base.

and doors (17), down to 13; as well as from behind the little theatre, by 20.

The smaller theatre was roofed, as we learn from an inscription, stating that the duumvirs, Caius Quintius and Marcus Porcius,[1] by a decree of the decurions, superintended the building of the covered theatre:

C QVINTIVS · C · F · VAL
M · PORCIVS · M · F
DVOVIR · DEC · DECR
THEATRVM TECTVM
FAC · LOCAR · EIDEMQVE · PROBAR

In front of the stage, of which the pavement is perfect, is inscribed, in bronze,

M · OCVLATIVS · M · F · VERVS · IIVIR · PRO · LVDIS[2]

This theatre, which has been imagined by some to be an Odeon, had also its privileged seats: the entrance to them was by the doors (18).

The cunei, of seventeen rows of seats, were approached by the great passage (20),[3] and doors (19), up a staircase, to the corridor at the back of the cavea.

It would seem that the portico (16) was a communication between the two theatres, for the use of the privileged.

Below the theatres was the great square, which, we are told by Vitruvius, should be thus contrived in their vicinity, for the reception of the audience, when bad weather

[1] The tomb between the two hemicycles, without the gate of Herculaneum, is probably of this Porcius, or of his father, who perhaps died just before the destruction of the city.

[2] The Austrian soldiers broke and materially damaged this inscription.

[3] This passage is full of inscriptions, scratched with nails and knives by people waiting for admittance. Amongst them is an ΑΛΕΞΑΝΔΡΟΣ. These were, of course, not always regulated by the strictest rules of propriety. They are very faint, and every day become less visible.

forced them to retire from their seats. Seventy-four columns, of the Doric order, disposed around an open area, formed an ample portico for this purpose; while under it were arranged cellæ, or apartments, amongst which were a soap manufactory, oil mill,[1] corn mill, and prison. An inner loggia (21) was connected with a suite of apartments (22). There was also an exedra (23).

This square is commonly called the Soldiers' Quarters.[2] The fluted columns are of coarse stone, coated with stucco, and coloured; two, in the centre of each side, are painted blue, the rest alternately red and yellow. The lower undiminishing portions of all, unfluted, are of a dark red; between each, seem to have been pedestals. On a column, near the centre of one end, is the figure of a soldier, or gladiator, scratched with a nail: and about are idly scrawled, in the same manner, names in Latin or Greek.

In the rooms around, skeletons were found, the decayed bones of the legs and arms retained by iron fetters. Pieces of armour, for the legs, thighs, and arms, were discovered in the exedra, in the middle of the east end, as well as helmets, ornamented with dolphins and tridents, in relievo, some incrusted in silver. On one was represented the principal events in the taking of Troy; others had vizors, gratings, or round holes to see through. From their size and weight, it has been disputed whether they were ever worn, or only intended for ornament or trophies. Sir W. Hamilton, who was present at their discovery, saw their linings, which have since fallen out or decayed: they were probably used in the theatre. Amongst other matters was a curious trumpet of brass, with six ivory flutes, all com-

---

[1] Cato says, the stones for these were brought from Pompeii and Stabia.

[2] Soldiers sometimes were quartered in the porticoes.—Tacit., 'Hist.,' 1, 31.

municating with one mouth-piece. The flutes were without holes for the fingers. A chain of brass hung to this instrument, for the apparent purpose of securing it to the trumpeter's shoulder.[1] It is now in the Museum.

24. Above the theatre is the temple of Isis, to which this is the entrance; over it was an inscription, now removed:

N · POPIDIVS · N · F · CELSINVS
ÆDEM · ISIDIS · TERRÆ · MOTV · CONLAPSAM
A · FVNDAMENTO · P · SVA · RESTITVIT
HVNC · DECVRIONES · OB · LIBERALITATEM
CVM · ESSET · ANNORVM · SEXS · ORDINI · SVO
GRATIS · ADLEGERVNT

25. The Ædes; for this little building is not called a temple. They differed, inasmuch as the former was not consecrated;[2] but the distinction was seldom attended to. And here, perhaps, was an affected humility in a worship scarcely tolerated.

The ædes was placed upon an elevated podium, like most others at Pompeii. In front was a Corinthian tetrastyle portico, of six columns. At the shoulders were two projecting pieces, with niches; behind one of which were steps, and a side doorway to the cell. The entrance from under the portico was wide, but the interior shallow, and a long pedestal for statues occupied its whole width. This was hollow underneath, with two low doorways.

Nearly opposite the entrance to the enclosed space was an ædiculum (26), covering the sacred well, to which was

---

[1] Ennius expresses its sound:

"At tuba terribili sonitu taratantara dicit."

[2] GELLIUS, 14, 7.—See Plate LXIX.

a descent by steps. On the pediment over the door, in stucco relievo, is a vase, with a figure on each side, in the act of adoration. Before this building was the only altar upon which sacrifice had been offered; its top was burnt, and the bones of the victims remained; while the wall of the adjoining building was discoloured with the smoke. Opposite this is the place for depositing the ashes of the victims.

There are several other altars, or pedestals, within this enclosure: on two, flanking the steps which ascend to the temple, were found the basalt Isiac tables, with hieroglyphics, now in the Royal Museum.

The area, in the midst of which the temple is placed, is surrounded by a covered portico of brick columns, of a species of Doric order, stuccoed. At their bases runs a gutter, to convey away the water falling from the roof. In an angle, a beautiful marble statue, about two feet high, of Isis, was discovered upon its pedestal.[1] The drapery was painted a tender purple, and some parts were gilt. She held a sistrum of bronze in the right hand; in her left, the Egyptian symbol,—the key of the sluices of the Nile. In a niche was also found a statue, usual to such temples,—Harpocrates, his fore finger upon his lip. Varro says, such statues were in all temples of Isis, to admonish that silence was to be observed. There were, also, Anubis, with a dog's head, Bacchus, Venus, Priapus; with paintings, utensils of bronze, and, in one of the chambers, a skeleton of a man, with a crow-bar, as if he had endeavoured to break his way out. The walls were highly ornamented in stucco, with paintings; which, as well as the statues, are now in the Museum.

---

[1] Inscribed,

L CÆCILIUS
PHOBUS · POSUIT

27. Saloon, paved with mosaic: in the pavement is—

N POPIDI CELSINI
N POPIDI AMPLIATI
CORELIA CELSA

28. Probably the keeper's apartments. In one room was found a skeleton; near it was a plate, on which were fish-bones; while the utensils used in cooking that fish were discovered in the kitchen (29).[1]
30 Was a room, with a bath.

We learn, from Tibullus, that prayers were offered to Isis twice a day. In the morning was the salutation, and morning sacrifice, upon opening the temple. In Arnobius, Apuleius, and Porphyry, the use that was made of fire and water is pointed out. Martial speaks of the evening service; when, after prayers, the temple was closed. The learned reader may find in Apuleius this ceremony, concluding with vows made at the door of the adytum, by the priest, for all orders of men; after which the people are dismissed in Greek,—the λαοις αφισις.

31. Room, in which were found Priapus, Bacchus, and Venus, with a magazine of terra cotta lamps, and implements of sacrifice.
32. The area to which this opened (see Plate LXXIV) was, in all probability, one of those open porticoes, or auditories, where philosophers taught. It must have been particularly subject to inconvenience from those whose love of practical jokes could prompt them to annoy these assemblies from the adjoining street.[2]
34. The pulpitum.

---

[1] Plutarch informs us, that the priests of Isis ate fish alone, and passed an austere life.

[2] "Ex his qui in porticibus spatiabantur lapides in Eumolphum recitantem miserunt."—PETRON.

Rhetoricians held their schools first in the porticoes of temples;[1] for learning was little cultivated in early times, and slaves were its professors; gradually understood, it came into increasing request. The orator systematically spoke from an elevated spot, and the children of people of the highest rank were sent hither for instruction;[2] although "Haud tamen invideas vati quem pulpita pascunt."

The schools, whether of the Grammaticus, Rhetor, Sophista, Juraticus, or Scholasticus, were usually in the vicinity of the Forum, or some public portico, into which the crowd of auditors poured when dismissed.[3]

This space is surrounded on three sides by a very diminutive colonnade, of the Doric order, 13 feet 3 inches wide. On the side next the temple of Isis is no portico, and the first column is placed only half an intercolumniation from the wall. At the opposite end is an exedra, or recess (35), and two rooms (36). There are two entrances: one from the street (33); another from the portico of the Greek temple. The latter, the steps show to have been much used.

37. Entrance to the court of the temple, called of Æsculapius. The reputation of this god could not have been high at Pompeii, or perhaps the inhabitants had little need of his care. Against the entrance was a covered space. The steps ascending to the adytum were the whole width of the court. Before them is an altar (39), upon which were found three terra cotta statues, of Æsculapius, Hygeia, and Priapus. The cell containing the pedestal for the statue was fronted with columns, of which only indications remain.

---

[1] Livy, 3, 44.—Suet., de Illust. Gram.

[2] Tacitus, de Orat.—Nero caused his verses to be publicly recited in the theatres and porticoes.

[3] "Ingens scholasticorum turba in porticum venit."—Petron.

Pl. 65.

Engraved by Chas Heath.

POMPEII.

ENTRANCE PORTICO TO THE GREEK TEMPLE.

40, 41 Are apartments for priests, and matters relative, perhaps, to the adjoining temples.
42. Entrance to the house (43).
44 Is the garden, or area domus, thereunto attached.
45. Another house, upon a lower level. It probably had an upper story, as a flight of steps leads up, through 46, to the garden (47). It was the residence of a sculptor; some of whose statues, begun upon, were found, with others finished; as well as unworked marble, ready, with chisels and other necessary tools for carving it.
48 Are lower apartments.
49 Behind the theatre was a cistern, and tower.

PLATE LXV.

View of the entrance, or propylea, to the area of the Greek temple.[1] Pieces of the columns and entablature are ranged within. It may be remarked, that the ancients rarely, if ever, placed these entrances opposite the front of their temples; but generally contrived that two sides of the latter should be presented to the first view.

[1] See the foregoing plan, wherein the fountain is marked 1.

PLATE LXVI.

This restored geometric elevation will give some idea of the foregoing, when perfect. The columns are 2 feet 1 inch in diameter, and about 17 feet 6 inches high, of black Vesuvian stone, stuccoed, and painted yellow: their distance apart averages 5 feet 5 inches. It will be observed, that, like the Greek, the circular base stands without a plinth, immediately upon the upper steps. The volutes are all angular.

PLATE LXVII.

View of the remains of the Greek temple, described at page 178.

Portions of two columns will be observed in their places. In the distance is Mount Lactarius, ending with the island Capræ. The fortified rock of Hercules, now Rivegliano, is seen in the sea.

Under Lactarius is Castel a Mare, not far from Stabia, where Pliny the historian was suffocated by the sulphureous vapour from Vesuvius, which is behind the spectator. Many beautiful monuments of ancient art have been there found, and removed to the Royal Museum; but the excavations are abandoned.

The semicircular seat is on the right of the steps of the

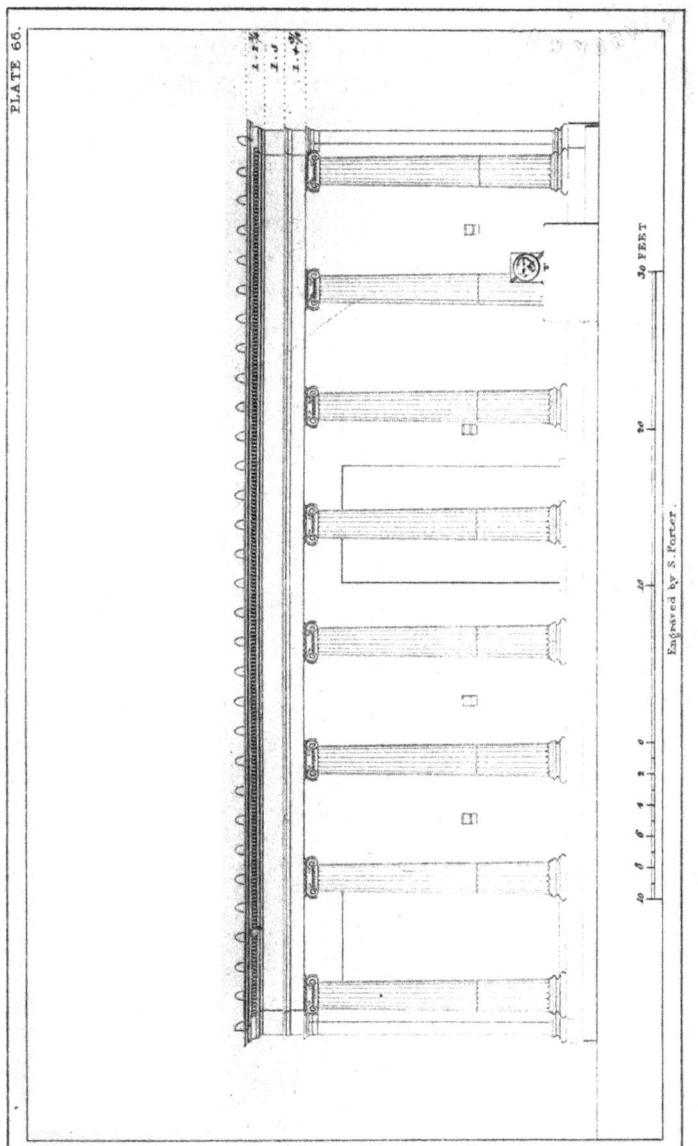

POMPEII.

ENTRANCE PORTICO TO THE GREEK TEMPLE.

POMPEII.

REMAINS OF THE GREEK TEMPLE.

temple. The puteal, and pen for victims, on the left. A capital of one of the columns is represented in the fore-ground.

The upper step appears to have been 53 feet wide; the length is not easy to ascertain, as it does not wholly remain, for the foundations are dilapidated to the right.

PLATE LXVIII.

View of the excavation, of which the plan is given, Plate LXIV. A part of the great wall of the larger theatre always was above ground, and should have enabled the diligent antiquary to ascertain the site of Pompeii. Between this wall, which has, however, been modernised, and the spectator, is the court of the temple of Isis. To the right the auditorium, and area of the Greek temple. The propylea, or entrance, to the latter will be observed at the farthest end of the street immediately under, in the view; in which is also the door to the auditorium, and that to the court of Isis. Behind this temple is the cistern, marked on the plan 49.

The end of the Greek temple and the pen for victims appear on the left, beyond the great theatre. The flight of steps (11) begins to descend from near that point; while, more to the left, is the square of the Soldiers' Quarters, and the taverna, under the trees.

To the left of the latter, in the distance, is Gragnano, and, to their right, Castel a Mare, both under Mount Lactarius, one of the projecting points of which upon the sea, is Saint Francesco di Paula. This mountain, celebrated by Galen for its mild and salubrious air, slopes down till it forms the promontory of Minerva.

The little theatre, from its position falling from the spectator, is not visible; but the temple of Æsculapius, with its altar, is nearly in the fore-ground.

It is not possible to describe every point of this plate; but the whole may be traced by reference to the plan, Plate LXIV. The general plan will also show the little building from which the view is taken.

PLATE LXIX.

This view will be explained by reference to page 185, and is taken from the entrance to the court.

Two more columns of the portico of the temple are without their capitals, as well as a part of their shafts. In the surrounding portico, a space as wide as two intercolumniations has been left, opposite the steps leading up to the cell; and pilasters, of a higher proportion than the columns, seem to have supported an arch, marking the centre.

This temple was amongst the first things found. It has been often drawn, and, we believe, always from the same point of view; while that point has been little explanatory of the whole. For the intention of making this plate more so, a broad liberty has been taken in removing great part of the four columns nearest the spectator, which in reality exist, like the others, entire. The whole is very small, and the Corinthian columns are not more than 10 feet high. The little entrance to the left is to the room (29).

POMPEII.

VIEW IN THE COURT OF THE TEMPLE OF ISIS.

POMPEII.

VIEW IN THE GREAT THEATRE, LOOKING TOWARDS THE SCENE.

Engraved by W. Lizars.

POMPEII.

PLATE LXX.

View in the great theatre.
This will be explained by reference to the plan. The Soldiers' Square, and little taverna, will be observed, as well as the hollow under the stage, mentioned page 181. The wooden floor of the stage would appear to have been upon a high level, compared with the orchestra. The doors in the white wall are to the scene and post-scene of the little theatre.

PLATE LXXI.

Back of the great theatre.
This view is taken from the top of the flight of steps (11), and shows the back of the scene, with the doors (12 and 17). Over the former is the temple of Isis.

PLATE LXXII.

Colonnade of the Soldiers' Quarters. The stuccoed columns were alternately painted red, yellow, or blue; the unfluted part always red. The gallery is restored, we are told, as pointed out by the carbon of the ancient wood-work. The angle represented is that next the taverna.

PLATE LXXIII.

Little theatre.

The only explanation that can be given to this view is to refer to the plan, Plate LXIV. The part to the left was covered over with the wooden floor of the stage. The bronze inscription ran upon the pavement in a straight line, connecting the two extremities of the lower semicircle of seats.

POMPEII.

COLONNADE BELOW THE GREAT THEATRE.

POMPEII.

VIEW IN THE LITTLE THEATRE.

POMPEII.

VIEW OF THE SCHOOL BEHIND THE GREAT THEATRE.

PLATE LXXIV.

View of the school behind the great theatre.

These slight columns are of a very agreeable proportion, though 8 diameters, or 10 feet 10 inches high; being 1 foot 4 inches at the base. They stand upon a step of 5 inches, next which is a channel, to receive the water falling from the roof. The abacus is 1 foot $7\frac{1}{2}$ inches square, and 3 inches thick: the intercolumniation 7 feet 6 inches.

The opposite entrance is from the portico of the Greek temple, of which some of the columns are seen.

The wall on the right, dividing this from the street, is very much higher than the columns.

The pulpitum is about 4 feet 10 inches high, and the die 2 feet 9 inches broad: its cornice projects 6 inches: before it is a pedestal, and behind a flight of steps, 5 feet 6 inches high. The whole advances forward into the uncovered space 10 feet. This latter was 29 feet 3 inches by 65 feet 6 inches.

PLATE LXXV.

View in the Amphitheatre.

The heroes of amphitheatres were always infamous; and never rose from that state, like the heroes of the drama, to be the companions of the rulers of the world. But the desperate valour of those condemned to the arena appears to have frequently called forth the admiration, or awakened the pity, of the spectators; while their manly exercises excited the emulation of the senators of Rome.[1] Madness must have prompted Caius; whereas the skill of Commodus, brutal in his enjoyments, and perfected by seven hundred combats, surpassed that of the most experienced gladiators; while his thirst for blood became more insatiate with each expiring victim.

The same division of orders obtained in the amphitheatre which took place at the theatre. That of Pompeii had 24 rows of seats, and has been said to be capable of containing 30,000 people: but this is an erroneous calculation, as it has not 20,000 feet of sitting room, and would consequently not admit more than 10,000. Neither can any conclusive argument with reference to the population of the city be drawn from this circumstance, when we recollect a passage before quoted: from which it appears, that the inhabitants of the neighbouring towns assembled here on the occasion of the shows. The population was, perhaps, under 20,000.

---

[1] One thousand senators and knights once appeared, in compliance with the wishes of Nero.

POMPEII.

VIEW OF THE AMPHITHEATRE.

Around the arena were paintings and a line of inscriptions. Amongst them we observe

C CVSPIVS · C · F · PANSA · PATER · DV · I · D
IIII QVINQ · PRÆF · ID · EX · D · D · LEGE · PETRON

C CVSPIVS · C · F · F · PANSA · PONTIF · D · VIR · I · D

Surrounding inscriptions:

MAG · PAG · AVG · F · S · PRO · LVD · EX · D · D

T·ATVLLIVS·G·F·CELER·H·V·PRO.LVD·LV·CVN·F·C·EX·D·D

At a gate is

C QVINCTIVS · C · F · VALC
M · PORCIVS · M · F · DVO . VIR
QVINQ · COLONIAI · HONORIS
CAVSSA · SPECTACVLA · DE
SVA · PEQ · FAC · COER · ET · COLO
NEIS · LOCVM · IN · PERPETVOM
DEDER ·

In the north entry to the arena, on the left-hand side, are nine places for pedestals, to form a line of separation, dividing the width into a wide and a narrow passage.

The shows, both of the theatre and amphitheatre, were under the superintendence of the edile, and were given either by public or private munificence. The gladiators of Ampliatus were brought forward to mark the funeral obsequies of Scaurus, whose tomb has been given in Plate VIII. Upon a wall in the basilica, there is evidence of another instance of their appearance, but in what year we are ignorant.

N · FESTI · AMPLIATI
FAMILIA · GLADIATORIA · PVGNA · ITER
PVGNA · XVI · K · IVN · VENAT · VELA

It was, perhaps, the 17th of May preceding the destruction of the city. This appears to have been a repetition of a previous combat; and we find at the door of the edile Svettius, upon a stone, which had been before used for similar notices, the information, that another repetition would be given on the 31st of the same month, exactly three months before the day of the first recorded eruption of Vesuvius; which, we are told by Dion, burst forth while the people of Pompeii were sitting in their amphitheatre.

PLATE LXXVI.

Painting, from the Amphitheatre.
This is evidently a preparation for combat. The tubista appears.

"Et tuba conmissos medio canit aggere ludos."

PLATE LXXVII.

Painting, or rather daubing, upon a wall, of the twelve gods; but curious, as exhibiting the "Consentes Dii majores gentium."
We have here Juno, Diana, Apollo, *Vesta*, Minerva, Jupiter, Venus, Vulcan, *Ceres*, Mars, Neptune, Mercury. They are all of the true ruddle god colour.
Under them are the *genii loci*. Juno has the pomegranate, and a blue robe. A yellow vest is given to Diana,

Engraved by F.C.Lewis.

POMPEII.

PAINTING IN THE AMPHITHEATRE.

POMPEII.

PAINTING OF THE TWELVE GODS UPON A WALL.

A, GRIFFIN.
FRAGMENT OF A PAINTING.
AT POMPEII.

who is particularly tall. The drapery of Apollo is red, as well as that of Jupiter. The hair of Venus is different from the rest, and her greenish robe more transparent. Neptune's drapery is blue: that of Mercury and Vulcan red.

From an inscription found upon the wall of the great passage in the baths of Titus at Rome, it appears that this mode of preventing nuisance was necessary in the *interior* of such buildings; though the *names* of the gods seem there to have sufficed. In the passage alluded to over an altar somewhat similar to that shown page 141.

> DVODECIM DEOS ET DIANAM ET JOVEM
> OPTVMVM MAXVMVM HABEAT IRATOS
> QVISQVIS HIC MINXERIT AVT CACAVERIT

VIGNETTES.

The Puteal, forming the subject of the vignette at the head of the Preface, is explained page 179.

The six following vignettes are one fourth the scale of the original pictures, of which twelve, painted upon dark grounds, were found, together with thirteen pieces of less merit, adorning the same chamber at Pompeii, in the year 1749. The whole have been already published in the learned and no less expensive work of the Academy of Naples.

PAGE 13.

A most beautiful and graceful figure. Her vest, of transparent yellow, is edged with blue; and her light hair, intermixed with pearls, is bound with fillets of white: she wears bracelets, and a necklace of gold. "Qualis fuit Venus Apuleius cum fuit virgo, nudo et intecto corpore, perfectam formositatem professa, nisi quod tenui pallio bombycino umbrabat spectabilem pubem."—See *'Ant. d'Ercol.'*

Page 17.

A female Centaur, bearing a green pallium, and holding a festoon, carries a Bacchante, robed in yellow, with the thyrsis. The equine portion of the former is white, and the head has horses' ears. Zeuxis was the first who imagined the female Centaur: the necessity of such beings having escaped the recollection of the poetic inventors of the male; always by them represented as of hideous countenance.

Page 47.

This no less beautiful figure holds the tambarine, which her right hand appears to have just struck. Her double necklace and bracelets are of pearls; her white vest is bordered with red, of which colour, also, are the ties of her sandals.

Page 61.

A Centaur, in full speed, with his hands bound behind, has the human portion a dark flesh colour, and the other of iron grey. He bears a Bacchante.

Page 87.

The fair hair of this figure is interwoven with leaves of an aquatic plant. Clad in a white robe, with a veil of green, in her right hand is a basket, while her left sustains a patera. She wears slippers.

Page 99.

This figure is clad in a white tunic partly covered by an upper garment of azure, bordered with red. Her ear-rings are pearls; her hair is bound with a red fillet, and restrained by a yellow veil. In her right hand is a branch, with citrons; her left holds a golden staff or sceptre, with an Ionic capital.

After many folio pages of learning upon these graceful figures, the Academy of Naples conclude with the reflection, that notwithstanding the many plausible conjectures they had thrown out, nothing certain could be asserted respecting them; for that it is in vain to attempt a system upon the *capricci* of the painter.

Page 60.

A cippus, explained page 78. It was, probably, painted with a likeness of the person it commemorates.

Page 98.

See page 93 for the description of this.

Page 107.

This representation of a Pompeian convenience is described page 123.

Page 141.

An altar at the angle of the street near the excavation of Queen Caroline, marked (a) on the great plan of the city.

The intention of these altars has been alluded to page 97 and 162. The prayer on making an offering may be seen in Plautus.—"Quæso te, ut des pacem, salutem, et salutatem nostræ familiæ."—*Mercator*, i, 4—12.

Virgil is uncertain whether the snake was the "geniumne loci, famulumne parentis."—*Æneid*, v, 95. The divine genius might assume various forms.

Page 143.

A shop, of which the counter is seen in shape of the letter L. In this were sunk and fixed large jars, to hold the materials for sale. In front of the counter, the shutters were slipped in a groove, and the closed door, fitted to the edge of the last, and, when fastened, kept all secure. The door was hung on pivots, and of course opened to the left.

Page 163.

This imitation of a ham was of bronze, silvered, and contrived as a portable sun-dial; the tail forming the gnomon. It is published in the 4th volume of the '*Antichita d'Ercolano*, where it is fully explained.

Upon the back of the ham are described seven vertical lines, under which are abbreviated the names of the twelve months, beginning with January, retrograding to June, and again returning to December.

IVN · MA · AP · MA · FE · IA
IV · AV · SE · OC · NO · DE

Seven other lines traverse the above, and, by their intersections with them, show the extension of the shadow thrown by the gnomon on the sun's entering each sign of the Zodiac; and, consequently, at every point in his path through the ecliptic. They likewise point out the hours of the day; the shadow descending with the rising, and again ascending with the declining sun.

The Academy observe, that in suspending, to make use of this instrument, the side should be presented to the sun; and when the extremity of the shadow of the gnomon reaches the vertical line marked with the name of the actual month, the horizontal intersection will show the hour. It is added, that it had been observed to act nearly correctly through the whole day: but it is not explained whether the instrument was made to turn with the revolving sun, without which it is evident that it could not have acted at all; and if so, it would appear to have been intended for momentary use, and to have required adjustment whenever made use of.

Page 165.

Picture of Bacchus and Silenus, referred to page 155. Bacchus and his followers covered the ends of their spears with the pine cone.[1] The aureolus encircling the head of the principal figure was sometimes put around the whole bodies of divinities:[2] though at first it was peculiar to the Sun, according to Orpheus, as cited by Macrobius; who also shows Bacchus to have been the same as the giver of light.

---

[1] Diod. and Ovid.
"Pampineis agitat velatam frondibus hastam."

[2] "Αυγη δ'ασπετος η, ανα δε δροσω αμφιμιγεισα
Μαρμαιρη δινησιν ελισσομενη κατα κυκλον
Προσθε θεου."

"Ηλιος ον Διονυσον επικλησιν καλεουσιν."

He is here represented as described by Euripides :[1] his long hair scattered about his shoulders, and, like that of both deities, uncut. His right hand holds the carchesium,[2] reversed, over a panther, one of the metamorphosed nurses of the god, according to Oppian, who says those animals are still fond of wine,

"Liber muliebri et delicato corpore pingitur."
ISIDOR.

The learned editor of the work upon the marbles in the British Museum remarks upon the epithet ωμαδιος, that Bacchus is usually represented leaning upon the shoulders of his followers.

The old man, bearded and bald, of whom half 'the distended abdomen' is concealed by white drapery, is, without doubt, Silenus.[3]

"Φαλακρος γερων σιμος την ρινα."

PAGE 173.

Soon after the first excavations, two bone admission tickets were found, in clearing the theatres. One roughly offers the view of the exterior of a theatre, with a door, half open, approached by an ascent of three steps; and to the right of the latter seems marked a railing, of the common Pompeian form. Upon the reverse is the name ΑΙΣΧΥΛΟΥ; from which circumstance it is imagined that the piece to the representation of which it admitted was Greek, and of the tragic poet Æschylus.

Upon the other tessera, a semi-circular edifice seems to represent the cavea of a theatre, divided into cunei: from the midst arises a tower. On the reverse is the word *hemicyclia*.

[1] BACCH., 455. [2] MACROBIUS, 5, 21. [3] LUCIAN.

The hemicyclia were probably the last rows next the orchestra, which in this theatre were wider than those above, and not, like them, divided by diverging flights of steps. Pollux mentions this as a part next the scene, and in the immediate vicinity of the orchestra.

In the 5th volume of the '*Ant. d'Ercolano*' will be found a learned dissertation, in explanation of these; various tesseræ are instanced, from which we see that the Greek letters B. Γ. H. I. IA. IB. were respectively accompanied by and synonymous to the Roman numerals, II. III. VIII. X. XI. XII. and the same may be observed in those before us. This fact serves to show, besides the peculiarity of this system with regard to the two last, that while Greek was the language used in the drama, and consequently that best understood by its frequenters, it was considered at the same time expedient to mark the places also in the language of the government.

The second ticket certainly points out a *place* in the theatre; and while the explanation of the learned Academy is submitted, analogy suggests the presumption that the *performance* was not meant in the first. The name of Æschylus offered an irresistible inducement to the learned Academy; but his works at this period had become antiquated even at Athens. We see in Aristophanes, *Acharn.* 25, that the first seats were called προτοζυλα; and, in Hesychius, ικρια is an appellation applied to the upper rows. It is strongly suspected that the real reading of this ticket is some Greek word, synonymous to the *mœniana* of the Latin, and that it was an admission to the gallery, constructed of wood.

Page 175.

Agamemnon and Achilles.

This painting is referred to page 157. It undoubtedly represents a scene in the opening of the Iliad, and the source of its action:

> "Achilles' wrath, to Greece the direful spring
> Of woes unnumber'd."

Minerva, sent by Juno, and visible only to Achilles, appears at the moment when, provoked by the overbearing tyranny of Agamemnon, the hero of the poem is no longer able to repress his indignation. The invisibility of the goddess is prettily expressed by concealing the greater portion of her person.

Page 199.

A ship, from a painting.

THE END.

www.ingramcontent.com/pod-product-compliance
Lightning Source LLC
Chambersburg PA
CBHW031421150426